Captivate

7 Secret Strategies
to **ATTRACT**
Dream Clients

TAYLOR SIMON

DD
PUBLISHING

Praise for
Captivate

"John Maxwell gave us the Laws of Leadership. Well, Taylor Simon has now defined the Laws of Captivation for us all! Using her strategies, you will learn how to grab and keep a captivate audience, and by doing so, take your business and lifestyle to the next level!"

Dr. Catrina Pullum
PRESIDENT OF PULLCORP MEDIA AND BUSINESS CONSULTING GROUP

"As a woman who's working to thrive and evole in musin, ministry, media and business, the genius of Captivate has ignited a fire in me that will help me blaze a new trail. This book is chocked full of insight, thorough information, and strategies that will set you on the right path to success."

Candy West
INTERNATIONAL GOSPEL RECORDING ARTIST

"Taylor's magnanimous mind brings together concepts of branding and marketing in such a strategic way that is has created for us the Laws of Captivation. These laws help businesses, organizations, and personal brands alike begin to take a journey that will transform the look, feel, and attrativeness of their brand. After reading this book, I literally feel energized and equipped to take the world by storm with my new branding savvy and marketing techniques!"

Alford D. Simon
MASTER COACH, AUTHOR, CEO + FOUNDER OF EMPOWERMENT COACHING

These pages are what your business and brand is begging for. One of the most brilliant creative minds of our time, Taylor shares with great passion 7 key secrets that anyone can implement right away! This essential guide is packed with practical insights on captivating and sustaining the attention of your audience and then some. It was an easy read and it is a great start for someone with little experience or years of experience in branding, marketing, or advertising your business. It will challenge, inspire, and equip you to do, think, and say things that you may not have done before. This book is truly a treasure.

Sonjia Pelton-Sam
THE GLAM COACH

Captivate: 7 Secret Strategies to *Attract*
Dream Clients

Copyright © 2017 by Taylor Simon

Cover Design by Divine Desires

Published by:
Divine Desires Publishing
P.O. Box 33200
Fort Worth, TX 76132
www.divinedesires.org

Printed in the United States of America

Divine Desires Publishing, 2017

ISBN-13: 978-0-9982512-1-9
ISBN-10: 0-9982512-1-6

PUBLISHING

Because of You...

My Heavenly Father...

You always push me to do things that I never thought that I could do. You never let me settle for safe. Sometimes I get so frustration when you stretch me to do things that make me feel uncomfortable, but I know that in the uncomfortable is where I need you the most. So thank you for pushing me beyond my fears. Thank you for streching me beyond my limits. Because of you I believe in the impossible, because of you I exchanged my fear for faith, because of you I think bigger, bolder, and braver, because of you I can choose progress over perfection. Thank you for the talents that you've given me to do crazy, unimaginable things with. This is one of the first of many gifts to the world that I so enjoy sharing for your glory. I couldn't do any of this without your strength. I pray that these words will touch You in the deepest way.

My Loving Husband...

My love, you are my best friend; you are my blessing; you are my King. I must confess, I feel the pressure when you are challenging me to be better, but I know that without the push I can't be greater. You bring the greatness out of me. You remove darkness out of me. You bring out the best in me. Because of you, I don't have to pretend, I don't have to fight to prove myself, I don't have to perform, I don't have to strive. Sweetheart, because of you, I feel like I am enough, in life, in business, in ministry, and eternally in love with you. So thank you for defending me and believing in me when I didn't believe in myself. Thank you for making me feel like the most beautiful woman in the world that creates beautiful things. Thank You for being my tech guy. Thank you for being my extra set of eyes. Thank you for your wisdom, your guidance, your honesty, and keeping me focused when my mind is on a bazillion other things. Thank you for coaching me to not let another day go by without pouring my heart out on these pages. This book would not have happened without you. You are the most amazing husband that I can imagine. I know that God is good because He gave me you.

My Family...

I know things have been crazy and wild and unnatural and all sorts of things during this time of my life. If only I can put into words the unimaginable things that the Lord has done for me. But throughout this journey, each of you have been a major influence in my becoming. Mom and Dad, because of you, I have an unshakable determination to achieve my dreams. Because of you, I have this uncommon ambition and an aggressive work ethic and discipline that leaves no room for being average. You both were my greatest inspirations to use this book as the beginning of a new legacy that will outlive me. Thank you for challenging me to become the best version of myself. Daddy Gene and Mama Sonjia, you two are jewels. I cannot thank God enough for your hearts that so willingly and unashamedly took me in. Thank you for your love and support. And all of you are the best grandparents in the world! Momo, I will never forget your words, that only what I do for the Lord will last. Thank you. Thank each of you for continuing to believe in me.

My Friends + Followers...

In every way, this is for you and because of you. With every word and every letter, from every sentence, to every paragraph, I thought of you. Thank you for appreciating my thoughts, my experiences, my passion, and my uncommon methods. This book came with a purpose, and that purpose is you. It is my eternal mission to lovingly challenge you to do extraordinary things that will increase your influence, income, impact, and inner belief through the power of Captivation. I have this outragoues belief in you to *Captivate* the masses and bless them with all the incredible gifts that you have to offer. I pray that my secrets become your source of infinite success in business, life, and......forever.

things
are
about
to
get
really
good!

Table of Contents

Every next level will demand a **Different You**

Introduction

Introduction

CAPTIVATION IS THE NEW COMMODITY

So many of us have big dreams, but we are too afraid to walk into them. Some of us want big businesses, but we don't have the resources to support our wants. Some of us want success, but our faith is too small to believe it can be achieved.

Before I started my own business, became a brand strategist and the CEO of a thriving brand development and marketing agency that attracts celebrity clients, and became a heavily sought after speaker, I did not have a strategy, I did not have any money, I barely had support, and I lacked confidence. The only thing I had was a dream; my ability to take something that was worth $10 and make it look like it was worth $1000; and an unusually creative eye. I had a passion for style and a childlike ambition.

I am someone who never imagined that I would be speaking on any stage for anybody. I was used to being behind the scenes on my computer, and managed to get by as a freelance photographer and graphic designer. What's strange is that, before any of the business and brand development venture came to be, I was an entertainer in the music industry. I was used to performing and singing on stage, touring with celebrities in front of large audiences, and dancing to a beat that I was familiar with, when suddenly, my passion changed.

I lost the courage to captivate.

The entertaining stage of my life had changed and I was afraid to show up for the stage that was set before me in the marketplace. I had known that being an entrepreneur or a business owner was a calling of mine since the age of 7 years old, but to be honest, I wasn't ready when the opportunity presented itself.

The thought of attracting anyone outside of my comfort zone or "celebrity clientele" at that time seemed impossible to me. Then I had to advertise my business by attending events and connecting with people that "I thought" would criticize me? "Nope. I'm fine." That was my excuse every time!

Have you ever thought that something was too impossible because you thought that you weren't worthy of it? Meaning, everyone else can captivate and convert their dream clients, but "I can't" because of x, y or z. Everyone else can be successful, give value, make money, and live a Taylor Made lifestyle that they've always dreamed of, but "I can't" because of this and that…

I believe that everyone creates excuses as to

why they cannot be or become who they were intended to be. At the same time, we will always have moments of insecurity. But I could not allow myself to get comfortable staying in that space. I didn't want to let my excuses have power over me.

Once I got to that point, I reevaluated what I wanted and what I needed to do to make my dream a reality.

If you want to make a difference right now, you have to make some changes.

Captivation starts with change.

I remember the time when I told my husband about a specific dream client that I wanted to attract. We were just getting started with my company. He just smiled in response, knowing that I am always thinking and talking about something much bigger than me. After I told him, I declared it again, and gained more confidence in just professing it aloud the second time.

Get ready for one of the most important secrets **drum roll please**.........I attracted my first dream client by speaking it into existence.

YES!

I'm sure you're thinking, *"What in the world does this have to do with captivating, and branding, and marketing, and growing my business and making money and such?"*…Give me a moment to show you…….

I eliminated the negative self-talk that told me I was not capable of captivating my dream clients and I shifted my internal and external dialogue. I stopped telling myself that it was too impossible and started manifesting the impossible into that which is possible. I understood that the first "like" I needed before any "Facebook like" was the like that I gave myself when I woke up every morning. I realized that my ability to stand out was valuable, powerful, and purposeful. I embraced my difference and appreciated my uniqueness because through my difference, I was able to impact the world like no one else could.

I changed my language to get a different result.

I went through an entire *mindset and motive shift.* My mentality changed, and yes, my motives changed. I started doing research on how to market my brand to effectively engage my dream clients and began applying what I had learned.

Even though I did not have enough money at the time, **I began to see myself where I wanted to be.**

I started to ***dress like a boss.***
I started to ***walk like an expert.***
I started to ***think like a multi-millionaire.***

And I started to strategically position my brand

with client-attractive content, graphics, and services that were impossible to resist.

I became consistent with my presentations and delivered them in excellence. I took actionable steps that navigated me toward my desired goal of captivating dream clients, converting them into paying clients, and ultimately, living the life of my dreams. Yes. You guessed it, the <u>law of captivation</u> begins with seeing what you want and speaking it into your reality. It is believing that nothing is impossible. Then, once you have mastered your thoughts and words, you can move forward with activating those words by executing them with innovative strategy! *This is where my secret strategies come in.*

Although I still have a great deal to learn, this journey has taught me so much that I could not keep all of its valuable secrets to myself. I want you to achieve those same results, no matter who you are, or where you are in life: Entrepreneur, speaker, author, business leader, CEO, creative artist, huge organization, company executive, or a start-up company; I want to give you the secret sauce as to how I was able to attract my dream clients.

Guess what? I am your biggest 'brand' fan. And I am willing to spill the beans and teach you how to **Captivate** and become a global brand that everyone is raving about.

There are about 300 million people starting

about 150 million businesses a day in the world. Every time you look around, someone is writing a book, becoming a life coach, creating a new product, or starting a blog. Some of which may be similar to your business or brand that you desire to start, or already have. Yes, there may be thousands of other coffee shops around the world, but to many people, Starbucks stands out the most. Starbucks cracked the code and found a powerful marketing strategy that made them stand out amongst the many neighboring coffee shops.

Once they found out what set them apart, they were able to Captivate their audience and drive them to becoming committed, craving customers. So think about it. What makes you attractive? Now I'm not just talking about your physical attributes as a human being; although, I'm sure you look quite ravishing. But I'm talking about what makes your brand or business capture the attention of your dream clients. What sets you apart from the rest? What makes you or your brand interesting? When people scroll through their social media, are they drawn by your compelling content, or do they put you and your business on the delete friend's list? Captivating your audience with a compelling presentation influences connection and converts them into consistent, craving customers. Now, before I share my secret sauce, I want you to get out a pen and start identifying what currently makes you and your brand radiate.

_____

_____

_____

In this guide, I will share *7 Secret Strategies* to captivate your target audience with an extraordinary delivery, compelling presentation, eye-catching content, and an unforgettable message that will have your dream clients rubber necking your timeline, website, products, and services. From the moment you open your mouth, you will captivate people. From the moment you enter the room, your presence will be breathtaking. You will also learn how to position yourself like a boss, engage your audience, and create a profitable brand presentation. You will master the art of building a captivating brand through easy step-by-step tips that will help you draw millions. You will also identify who you need to become to attract what you want in your brand or business!

Get ready to go from undiscovered to unforgettable and learn the importance of creating a client-attractive brand to move your business and life in a powerful, positive and profitable direction!

Every next level of your life
will demand a
Different you.

@iamtaylorsimon #captivate

Professional Photos
attracts
Professional
People

@iamtaylorsimon #Captivate

SECRET
Strategy
#1

#1

Picture Perfect People

"A PICTURE IS WORTH A THOUSAND WORDS"

When it comes to captivating your target audience, high quality photos are essential. Always, and I mean always, invest in high quality photos. This ranges from professional portraits to professional stock photos.

If you want to be taken seriously, start engaging your dream clients with professional photos that reveal the best qualities of your brand image. Making this minor adjustment will make a huge difference when attempting to connect with thousands of viewers.

Let's start with an illustration that I'm sure most people can relate to: food photography. Have you ever browsed through the Google search engine to find a restaurant with hundreds of blurry, poorly lit photos? Or what about the occasional photos that you see on your Facebook timeline of "Aunt Shirley's Kitchen" that is meant to look like beef stew and cabbage on a styrofoam dinner container, but due to poor presentation, it looks like pig slop. I know that may seem a little dramatic, but let's be honest, don't you want to eat food that looks good to eat? I don't know about you, but if my food is not visually stimulating, I immediately assume that it will not taste good. Although these business owners display a level of determination and hope, these are some desperate attempts to frantically snap a photo in the heat of the moment. Trying to save money and time to gain business fast has its downfalls.

This same idea is for your business or your brand. Think about what you're communicating to your potential customers. If your pictures communicate, "I look cheap", you will attract clients that will respond saying, "I want cheap". Your dream clients will immediately expect less value when they see less effort to deliver your product or service because you failed to use professional photos.

Making it obvious that you took the cheapest route will drive cheap results.

@iamtaylorsimon #Captivate

I was born for spontaneity, but spontaneous efforts without an effective plan can turn into a disastrous outcome. Low quality photos translate to low quality services and products. Am I saying that you need to pay thousands of dollars to style your products or personal brand? No. I am simply stating that having professional pictures will position you as a professional person.

Improving your photos with great lighting, appealing angles, and high definition quality will increase your chances of attracting customers who value quality and will be willing to pay for it. Know that you are worth it!

Stock up on Stock Photos

When you are in need of some professional photos to represent your business or brand, you have the option to use your own; or of using unique stock images. Stock photos are professional images that anyone can purchase on a royalty-free basis for commercial design purposes. It is one of the most widely used components that companies use for marketing, creative, or educational purposes.

Stock photos can be used multiple times and is used for blogs, magazines, book publishing, business reports, advertising, web design, graphics design, television, film, interior design, and much more. The quality of stock photos is impeccable and is suitable for upgrading your brand presentation. Although most stock photos are not free, there are tons of free and affordable stock image websites that I would recommend.

Here's a list of free stock photo websites you can use to get started. In little to no time, you will have a portfolio full of professional images to effectively serve as a representation of your brand.

1. Picjumbo
2. Kaboompics

3. Unsplash
4. Pixabay
5. Pexels
6. StockSnap.io

Here's a list of my favorite affordable stock photo websites with premium images:

1. AdobeStock
2. Shutterstock
3. Deposit Photos

TIPS ON USING STOCK PHOTOS

Tip #1
Have you ever seen some of your friends or followers using the same images? Ever went to someone's website and said, "Hey, haven't I seen that image before?" Most of the time, you will find the most popular images first on a stock image website. Although the images may seem perfect for what you plan on doing, this is an indicator that those images have been used by a lot of people. One of the most awkward Internet moments, is finding another business using the same images that you have on your website. Not cool. There are tons of other images on various stock photo sites and I guarantee that you will be able to find many that would fit what you are trying to do.

Tip #2
Go big or go home. When using stock images, choosing the bigger file size is always the better bet. Always download the largest size, not just for Internet usage, but to meet your other needs.

Tip #3
Filtering your images based upon the purpose of your topics, marketing plan, or business or brand visual vision will help you to narrow down all of the zillions of photo options. I don't know about you, but for me, seeing all those images can be quite overwhelming. However, if you tackle this task with a plan, you are surely destined for efficient success. For instance, if you are in the beauty industry and want to create an ad to post on social media, you would type in the search bar "beauty, beautiful, fashion, make-up, gorgeous, etc.". Doing this will help you to minimize the time spent on rummaging through thousands of images.

Tip #4
Create a folder for your website, blog, or social media platform to organize and label all stock images that are relevant to each topic or subject. Specifically, you would arrange all "animal" stock images in one separate folder and "children" stock images in another. It sounds like a ton of work, but trust me, it will save you a ton of work when you are pressed for time when developing a marketing plan. Take some time to organize your images. It will be worth it in the end. You'll see.

Hit the Millions

Professionally rendered photos can also be classified as images taken with great lighting and with high-quality imagery that is crisp and clean. While selfies are great for capturing a memorable moment or flaunting off your new hair, cell phone images taken for business purposes should be handled with care and much professionalism.

Lighting is everything. Lighting plays a key role in the outcome of a perfect photo and selfies are no exception.

As I tell some of my clients in photo shoots, "always find the light". When taking photos, make sure you are facing the light. If you are inside, finding natural light is essential for capturing the perfect shot.

Slouching in your image tends to make anyone's image much larger than it is. Instead, always stand or sit with a straight spine, slightly raised chin, and relaxed shoulders. Following these simple steps will ensure that you will take pictures with angles that pleasantly capture an elongated posture, beautiful features, and your unique frame. Taking images of an up-close nose portrait or the top of your forehead on your phone would not be the best route to go.

In the same way, being mindful of your wardrobe, hair, facial hair, and makeup will also assist you in determining the specific audience that you would like to Captivate™. We will get into more detail about your appearance in the following chapters. Besides that, don't forget to be yourself. Whether you are taking professional headshots, a portrait photo shoot, or selfies, always be yourself and show your personality. People love connecting with people, not robots. Don't be afraid to smile and show that bright personality of yours. Attracting your dream clients with professional photos will position you as an expert in your industry.

Positioning yourself with professional pictures will convince onlookers that you have hit the millions.

@iamtaylorsimon #Captivate

Your audience will no longer have a reason to scroll past your profile or website because it invites them with a person that could potentially influence them. **Always remember, in your business, *your highest level of success is determined by your clients' perception of you.***

Take a Step

Although casual selfies are appropriate for personal profiles and pages; sophisticated, professional photos are considered to be more appropriate for public figures. Delivering professional photos does not always necessarily mean that you MUST be in a professional studio. (Although, you should always have a reasonable amount of studio quality photos from a professional photographer).

However, taking a simple step to invest in professional quality photos will increase your brand influence and attract leads.

Hire a local photographer who can display your product in the best way possible, or purchase a few stock photos with a positive message. After that first wonderful impression, your dream clients will be more captivated to know your story, check out your products and make that purchase.

You *spend your most valuable time, money, blood, sweat and tears on your business. Show it.*

PRESENTATION MOTIVATION

Have you ever been to a presentation and almost had to catch your big head bowling over towards the floor? What about claiming to "rest" your eyelids only to eventually scare yourself from a silent snore?

Let's be honest.

I'm sure you've never experienced a ton of exciting presentations in your lifetime. In fact, most of them are downright boring and lack "the it factor". Some presentations start off with fire and during mid-sentence become this faint, annoying background sound that some people ignore.

Overwhelming people with content can drown out the motivation to implement what is being delivered.

@iamtaylorsimon #Captivate

Without the bells and whistles to wake the people up, you will drown out the potential to develop interest. Now I'm not going to go into all the juicy details about establishing an absolute perfect presentation (I will share that with you later). However, in this case, I will share an effective approach to motivating your dream audience with visually stimulating imagery.

The No Show Slideshow

Microsoft PowerPoint. To all my Microsoft PowerPoint Scholars who still lists "MS PowerPoint expertise" as a skill; please retire this skill unless you are planning on elevating your craft to impact more viewers.

Yes, I get it. This software is easy to use and is compatible on most computers. Trust me, I understand. But I believe that some people misuse PowerPoint when attempting to create presentations that motivate. When it comes to motivating professional people to invest in your passion, most of the focus should not be on words crowding each slide.

Copying and pasting your notes on each PowerPoint slide, and reading them word-for-word aloud can get annoying. If you are reading this book, I would assume that you are a business professional, entrepreneur, speaker, or leader of some sort. With that being said, most of your audience will know how to read, so don't bother wasting your time. Instead, use relevant pictures, charts, graphs, and infographics.

Versatility increases your capacity to captivate without using a ton of words.

@iamtaylorsimon #Captivate

Leave room for your impressive communication skills to lead you into amplifying your message. No more no shows! Get ready to be surprised at how many dream clients show up to your next presentation because of your willingness to present with visuals that motivate. I know you can do it!

Display With Discretion

When considering what type of imagery to use in a PowerPoint, you should always remember to display with discretion. In other words, do not display visuals that are offensive, even if you secretly think they're hilarious. During your presentation, take your audience on a journey that makes them vulnerable to opening up, not through a nightmare that scares them back to sleep.

Although some photos are necessary, not all of them are effective enough to get your point across.

Relevant images that emphasize your point with humor are essential to sparking interest. If it makes sense, use it and liven things up. While you're at it, add a touch of color. Using slides in black and white can tend to hurt your eyes. Well, at least mine. Color captures attention. Bring your presentation to life by incorporating your brand colors, or vibrant colors that stand out and guides people to where you want them to go. Creating a great balance of color along with black and white will make your presentation easy on the eyes.

Use bold imagery and colors that will attract and not distract.

@iamtaylorsimon #Captivate

Pictures have an interesting way of shifting the mood in the room. Captivating your audience takes patience, persistence, and a little playful humor. Placing a cute or humorous image on every two slides will reinforce spontaneity. If you overwhelm your slideshow with images on every slide, your viewers will know what to expect. But if you diversify for presentation, you will win them by the element of a pleasant surprise. Interestingly, faces, babies, cute animals (puppies, kittens, or baby monkeys), emojis, icons, and memorable characters are popular visuals that capture your audience's attention.

People remember faces and symbols before remembering words. Most people remember the way someone made them feel before determining to make an investment. Using these powerful tools will quickly bring your presentation to life. Without a doubt, your presentation will leave a lasting impression on your audience when you make these subtle adjustments.

Awaken the Crowd

After surprising them with your charismatic personality, always bring them back to the heart of the conversation. You want them to walk away with valuable content, but you don't want to leave them without an engaging presentation. Challenge yourself to awaken the crowd by playing with emotion, colors, compelling visuals, and of course, your charismatic personality.

Dare to Be
Unforgettable

Be Spontaneous

Be
YOU

SECRET
Strategy #2

#2

Be Unforgettable

When you think about the Coca-Cola brand image, what initially comes to mind? Besides remembering the great taste of Coke, we are usually reminded of the bold, red script font written on the front of the soda can. Why is that important and what does that have to do with remembering who you are?

Well, it's quite simple.

Without physically having a Coca-Cola in your hand, you were able to visually identify their brand image instantly. It was easy for you to capture the visual elements of the Coke brand. The red, the script, the bold, and of course, the taste captivated you whether know it or not. The Coke brand psychologically caught your attention, captured you as a brand fan, connected with your pockets and converted you into a loyal customer. This, my friend is called the power of consistent brand awareness. Just like we remember the Coke brand, it is possible for the world to remember YOUR brand.

Every company or business has a brand, whether they see the value in it or not. In it's simplest form, a brand is who you are and how the world sees that. Visual branding elements such as a logo, business cards, websites, marketing collateral, social media presence, and advertising reflect who you are, and are supported by your messaging. These visual elements influence how people perceive or remember you, or your brand.

Brand consistency requires visual cohesiveness on every platform that displays your brand.

@iamtaylorsimon #Captivate

Crashing Collateral

Yes, this means ditch the busy blue and green colors on your business card with a floral design that does not complement your purple, black, and yellow car themed website. If the pattern concept on your website is zigzag, the pattern on your letterhead should reflect the same concept. Displaying a consistent design concept across all marketing collateral will help your dream clients clearly identify who you are. The last thing you want to do is confuse your potential clients.

Consistency eliminates confusion.

@iamtaylorsimon #Captivate

If your business card says "cutting-edge", "high-quality service", "committed to excellence", "innovative", "the best", your brand design should not contradict the messaging that is given. You will confuse your audience. Having a professional design that is consistent with your brand messaging will enhance your dream clients' perception of you. Don't damage your first impression by delivering marketing collateral that does not support your valuable product or service.

Delivering crashed collateral can harm your credibility.

@iamtaylorsimon #Captivate

When your potential leads do not see value, they will assume that your service or product lacks value. The way your audience perceives your brand plays a significant role in purchasing decisions. Your marketing collateral is the face of your company; and your marketing collateral is a tool that drives sales. How you present that will determine whether or not your dream client will invest in you. Always remember, if you commit to consistency, you will see the cash.

Keeping your overall brand theme consistent instills confidence and conveys professionalism, purpose, and stability. Once you have created your brand colors, logo marks, and additional brand elements, it is essential for you to develop a clean, consistent, matching theme that everyone can remember. Now this does not mean that you cannot be innovative, however, there is no point in spending extra money on a brand revamp when no one notices that you revamped. Don't mistake consistency as being boring, because consistency paves the way to creative impact.

THE CREATIVE SOLUTION

Establishing consistency is ultimately in the heart of your brand style guide. A brand style guide is primarily the visual blueprint for your business. This guide sets the creative direction and visual standard for your company. Inconsistency becomes irrelevant with this precious guide. Without one, you are bound to walk outside of its effective parameters and eventually fail to deliver an unforgettable brand. Your brand style guide is a go-to reference that you, graphic designers, illustrators, and publishers can refer to when developing a design, advertisement, or creative literature for your business. It ensures brand consistency throughout any collateral you produce, no matter who creates it.

Brand style guides contain all the necessary information to create whatever your business needs. Whether it be a website, advertisement, online communications or whatever else, this guide makes life easier. In addition, this document contains the specific visual ingredients on how all tangible elements of a brand (business cards, brochures, packaging, signage, etc.) should be used and communicated. This jewel is the visual DNA for your brand.

Staying on point with your branding calls for strong and strategic methods for keeping consistency.

@iamtaylorsimon #Captivate

Brown Paper Bag

So what's in this cool brand style guide? This visual brand style guide houses all relevant fonts and typography, colors, icons, patterns, styles, primary, secondary, and alternate logo concepts, and sometimes logo guidelines that represent your brand. Authenticity is crucial when keeping things consistent. Managing the perception of your company through these guides serves as a powerful force that sustains authenticity.

Serving your potential clients and leads takes an intentional effort to prevent a counterfeit image from circulating. In other words, without a brand style guide, your business becomes vulnerable to being unrecognizable. Now, I'm sure you're not an imposture. (Or at least, I hope not) And I would pray that you don't walk around with a brown paper bag around your head with cut out eyeholes.

This same idea can translate to your business or brand. If you are frequently delivering random colors and design concepts that have nothing to do with the visual identity of your brand, your business is walking around with a brown paper bag on it. No one can see who you are and no one is able to clearly recognize what you do. It's like getting a call from an unknown number. I don't know about you, but if do not recognize the number, sometimes I will not answer. Or it's like seeing an advertisement on social media of your friend's business event and completely ignoring it. Why is it ignored? Because there are too many random colors and a questionable logo that does not represent the original brand content most recognizable to you.

This brown paper bag covering the real identity of your brand prohibits viewers from perceiving your business as being reliable and authentic. Although they can see that someone is managing your business through the cut out "eyeholes", they are not able to accurately depict the message given. I call this "brand deception". Managing your business with a brown paper bag gives off a deceptive tone that pretty much says to your client "all I want is your money and I don't care about developing a relationship with you, or positioning myself as a worthy, credible investment". Your dream clients cannot build trust with a brand they do not know, or better yet, one they cannot vividly see through the crowd. And with this brown paper bag covering your potential, it deceives those who are willing to invest in your business into believing that value is unnecessary and lasting client relationships are optional.

This brown paper bag basically gives off the impression that you have something to hide and don't want anyone to know who you are. This behavior is also for those who are more consistent with changing up styles each week rather then sticking to the blueprint to build brand recognition and credibility. In addition, it implies that you're not interested in people identifying your brand and you would rather settle for making the minimum amount and being forgotten.

The brand covered with random creative fluff is the brand waiting to be revealed in order to make maximum impact.

@iamtaylorsimon #Captivate

If you're comfortable with delivering content that does not authentically represent the visual DNA of your brand, then look forward to a decline in consistent engagement. For instance, if your brand style guide exudes a royal theme, everything that is published to the public should reflect that same theme. Resist the urge to test the waters with a new concept and put your brand on demand with a purposeful brand strategy. Posture your brand presentation with purpose so that you can increase profitability. Your brand is waiting to be revealed. Don't settle for inconsistent methods. Get your brand style guide and show the world what you're made of.

Why is No One Using It?

So, if this guide is so important, why isn't everyone using it? Well, simply put. It's time.

For most people, time is money. And while one person is creating their brand identity style guide, the other is developing their sales strategy. Now I'm not saying that creating a crisp sales strategy is bad for business. But it becomes bad for business when business starts booming and you have to frequently explain your brand guidelines verbally rather then with a pre-made visual guide. How long does it take you to explain to a designer the vision behind your brand theme, and how are they not supposed to change any of the colors? What about finding every font you use and having to relay this to them as well?

Gaining a greater return on your investment is quantifiable when you do the hard work first, so that you can have fun later.

@iamtaylorsimon #Captivate

In a microwavable society, there are those who would rather throw something together than prepare and strategically plan for infinite success. Throwing things together always ends in chaos and confusion. Do yourself a favor and go with a guide. It will save a lot of frustration and miscommunication down the road.

Set Apart

Setting yourself apart is common when developing this guide. Because not a lot of people value this concept, this is your opportunity to exchange all bad habits to this brand new habit that will help you to stand out from the rest of your competitors.

Color Coded Brand

Colors are a distinctive way to convey your product and express the unique personality of your brand. It is one of the most noticeable, tangible, elements in your brand. Color further emphasizes how a brand is perceived and received. In addition, it helps with brand recognition and impressiveness, and has the potential to captivate your dream clients and readers. Color is a powerful communication tool used by designers to motivate action, influence mood, and spark emotions. As I've briefly stated before, bold brand colors have impact. It puts colors into context. Also, colors are a tool that is used to capture your audience's attention. Used effectively, you can get them to see what you want them to see, feel what you want them to feel, and do what you want them to do.

In fact, research reinforces that 60% of people will decide whether or not they're attracted to a message based on color alone. How you use color also affects the visibility of your brand and reinforces brand recognition by up to 80%.

Many of the most recognizable brands in the world rely on color as a key factor in their instant recognition. For instance, people are able to easily detect that a blue McDonalds sign is either a fake or viewed as an unannounced color change. Honestly, if I were to notice a blue and orange McDonald's sign, I just might stop to see what's going on. Most people know that the McDonalds logo has a yellow M on a red background. People see color before they recognize anything else.

When picking your color palette for your brand, make sure you stick with it. Colors can be easily changed from designer to designer or program, to program, to program. There are tons and tons of different hues, tones, tints, and shades of colors that you can choose for your brand. With that being said, it is important to have exact HEX codes for web and CMYK values and Pantone colors for printed items. Hex codes are the social security numbers for your specific colors. This unique combination of 6 numbers or letters contributes to the distinctive look of your brand.

Your Hex code will look like this: #000000

Usually, designers understand how this effective tool works and are able to translate it to meet the colors of your choice. With these specific colors codes, your brand colors remain unmatched and unduplicated because no one else would have your exact color: Unless you decided to share your brand style guide with the world, (which I do not recommend).

Color Psychology

Your unique combination of colors will promote brand consistency and recognition. If you want to create a color palette that attracts your dream clients and accurately represent your brand, you must have a basic understanding of color psychology.

So before you get into your creative flow, take a look at some color associations that will help you choose which works best for your brand.

Yellow is a go-to color for positivity, happiness, and warmth. This color is attention-grabbing (which explains why taxis are yellow) and it can also represent caution (think about yield-signs and traffic lights). Yellow is also viewed as being spontaneous and unstable. This color is a great color for call-to-action buttons.

Some common associations with yellow include caution, cheerfulness, cowardice, curiosity, happiness, joy, playfulness, positivity, sunshine, and warmth.

Blue is perceived as trustworthy, loyal, dependable, and serene. It's a popular color with financial institutions (IBM, Citibank, Bank of America, Chase) and social media sites (Facebook, Twitter, LinkedIn) due to its message of stability and trust. Blue is also a popular color for promoting products related to cleanliness (water purification filters, detergents), air and sky (airlines, air conditioners), and water and sea (cruise lines, bottled water). This color is usually avoided in restaurant logos and food packaging because it's said to suppress appetite. Studies have also shown that blue is the preferred color of men.

Some common associations with blue include authority, calmness, confidence, dignity, loyalty, success, security, serenity, and trustworthiness.

Green is the color of nature. It symbolizes growth, freshness, serenity, and healing. It also has a strong emotional correspondence to safety and balance. Darker greens are commonly associated with money, banking, and wealth, while lighter greens have a calming effect. Green has a positive association with productivity and sparks creativity.

Some common associations with green include freshness, faith, stability, harmony, health, eco-friendliness, healing, inexperience, money, and nature.

Purple is closely associated with royalty, nobility, luxury, wealth, spirituality and extravagance. It's a very rare color in nature, and many relate it to creativity and mystery. It is also said to stir up feelings of nostalgia.

Some common associations with purple include fantasy, mystery, nobility, ambition, power, confidence, dignity, royalty, imagination, and sophistication.

Red is the color of fire and blood, so it's often associated with energy, war, danger, and power but also affection, passion, desire, and love. It's an emotionally intense color, has very high visibility, and is often used to grab viewers' attention (think red tag clearance sales and "buy now" buttons). Red has also been known to raise people's blood pressure and stimulate appetite, so it's frequently used by food industry brands like Nabisco, Kellogg's, Frito Lay, Heinz, McDonald's, and Chick-fil-A.

Some common associations with red include action, adventure, aggression, blood, danger, drive, energy, excitement, love, passion, and vigor.

Orange is less intense than red but still packs a lot of punch; it communicated high energy and warmth. Like yellow, orange is also associated with joy, sunshine, and playfulness. You often find it used in logos to stimulate emotions or even appetites. (Watch out if you're hungry!) Orange can be used for fruits, sporting events, and board games.

Some common associations with orange include creativity, enthusiasm, determination, fascination, courage, attraction, success, encouragement, lightheartedness, affordability, and youth.

Pink is a feminine color that conjures feelings of innocence and delicateness. However, bright and vibrant shades of pink often evoke a bold and modern appeal. Pink also has a calming sensation (think about the Pepto-Bismol pink). Pink is a sign of hope (Breast Cancer Patients). Overall, pink is known for its friendly and light-hearted effect.

Common associations with pink include gratitude, romance, gentleness, nurturing innocence, softness, and appreciation.

Brown indicates nature and utility and is often used in logos related to construction and law due to its simplicity, warmth, and neutrality.

Common associations with brown include depth, earthiness, roughness, richness, simplicity, seriousness, subtlety, and utility.

Black represents power, elegance, sophistication, and authority. It's often associated with intelligence, but it's also associated with evil and grieving. It's a serious color that evokes strong emotions. Black is commonly seen: professional attire, luxury products, and limos.

Common associations with black include authority, class, distinction, formality, mystery, secrecy, seriousness, elegance, and tradition.

Breaking Color Tradition

Some brands break color traditions. T-Mobile's magenta (hot pink) is an unexpected color in the crowded cellular communications marketplace. As risky as it is, it does succeed in creating a unique brand identity. Of course, T-Mobile has a skilled team of marketing professionals to position their visual brand identity effectively.

You can do the same thing with your brand. But do this only if it makes sense to the message you are trying to convey. Use these color associations as a guide to aid you in selecting a combination of colors that captivate.

Creating Your Color Combination

After reading the color associations, now its time to create the color palette for your brand style guide. Strive to create a color palette that authentically speaks your brand messaging and the exact look and feel that you desire your brand to evoke. Creating a distinctive color palette for your brand starts with gathering color inspiration and pulling at least 4-6 colors from that inspiration.

Pinterest is the perfect tool for gathering inspiration. To begin, create a "Brand Colors" secret board and start pinning patterns, colors, and inspirational images that stick out to you. Try searching things like "branding, logos, or color palette" to get started. As you find things that gravitate to you, make sure you are looking for color similarities and inspirational images that are appropriate for the overall aesthetic of your brand. This may take some time. But for all the creative ones out there, be careful, because it is easy to get distracted and lose track of time.

Once you have gathered inspiration, now it's time to pull out at least 4-6 colors for your color palette. You can master this task through Adobe Color CC. I absolutely love using this tool. It's simple and easy to use. The eyedropper tool is especially useful for pulling colors from your collection of inspiration photos.

Adobe Color CC is another helpful resource that allows you to look through different color variations, create/save color palettes, and glance through preexisting color palettes for inspiration. And guess what? It also calibrates hex and RGB codes for you to save for your brand style guide.

Keep in mind, that the colors you choose at this point are just a start. They don't have to be your final colors. Trust me, you'll continue to revise and refine your colors as you go and grow comfortable with using these tools.

Why So Many Colors?

It's always good to have different color variations to choose from for each piece of marketing collateral, logo variation, website page, or social media ad. Depending on the aesthetics you are trying to achieve, it is always good to determine 2-3 primary colors and 4-5 secondary colors. You will use the 2-3 primary colors more often then the 4-5 secondary colors used as accent colors.

Of course, you don't have to use all of these colors. You can even feel free to add more. Your color palette is an extremely important element in your brand style guide. Use this color combo to visually communicate a message that will inspire your audience to take action. Just have fun with your color exploration and prepare to captivate your dream clients with a unique color identity.

A Timeless Font

Using a specific set of fonts that reflect the individuality of a brand is essential to achieving a universal tone of voice, and greatly improves brand awareness and legibility. Selecting a typeface that is distinctive, memorable and recognizable can trigger your audience's attention. It influences the way consumers feel and forms an emotional connection between the typeface and the brand experience it represents.

Typefaces come in multiple weights and styles and can be stylized in different ways (e.g. uppercase/lowercase, bold, italics), which can affect the feel of your marketing materials. Defining which typefaces are used, and how is another way to define how your company's materials look. Captivate your audience with a timeless font that they will never forget.

Other Components

Other common brand style guide components consist of the following:

- Primary, Alternate, and Secondary Logos
- Icons
- Web Styles (buttons and iconography)
- Copywriting style
- Brand images and inspiration

An Innovative Approach

Each element of your brand style guides reinforces brand consistency and keeps things clear and concise. It's important to note that brands can change. However, this guide will set the foundation for your visual communication, allow flexibility, and provide something to look back to. Include this innovative approach to developing consistent branding across all platforms. You want to keep this in mind so that you can be easily remembered, rather than easily forgotten.

A THOUSAND EMPTY WORDS

You only have a few seconds to captivate your customers. So make your first impression unforgettable.

@iamtaylorsimon #Captivate

Of course, consistency in your brand goes beyond logo design, colors, and a brand style guide. For example, the messaging and design elements on your website should always align with your marketing efforts. Confusion kills the charm. If your website isn't clear and is not consistent with your vision and value statements, your brand message will not stick. You only have a few seconds to captivate your customers and the last thing you want to do is confuse a potential client. Those few seconds are crucial and once engaged, you want to create a lasting impression. You can have a thousands words on your website, social media presence, marketing collateral, blog, advertisements, or brand elements, but if your messaging does not correlate with your overall vision, your words are meaningless and empty.

World Class Customer Satisfaction

Consistency is the key to client satisfaction. Have you ever went to your local grocery store only to be pleasantly overwhelmed by tons of smiling employee faces? Or what about the cashier that is always happy and you're still trying to figure out why they are so happy? I mean, could anybody really be that happy? As if every day was filled with sunshine and roses? After an encounter with this person, you have no other choice but to buy a few snickers at the register just because they asked.

It's called the power of consistent customer service. As you walk through the glass sliding doors, to your surprise a rolling grocery basket meets you. Then, as you get ready to tackle your grocery list, an employee asks how your day is going, and politely offers you some free samples. This behavior doesn't just stop at the door. It never ends.

It's about being absolutely obsessed with constantly delivering the best customer experience possible. It's about delighting each client whenever they interact with your organization. You become a brand magnet when you provide value-adding products and services, competitive prices, and exceed expectations. It's about being driven by passion, purpose, and genuinely caring for your clients. Delighting your leads and clients requires respect, authenticity, simplicity, and never-ending improvement processes. You delight your clients when it's no longer about making a profit, but it's about servicing the people.

Engaging your dream clients is not just about follow-up, it's about following through. Following up consistently and following through enduringly.

@iamtaylorsimon #Captivate

There is nothing more gratifying then staying in constant contact with your clients and remaining true to your word throughout the process. It's not just about writing down a set of core values, but putting them to action in real time.

The unforgettable companies listed below are the ones that have mastered the concept of delivering customer experience consistently. I hope that what they have to say will inspire you in some way!

Disney
"Our aim should be to always exceed our Guest's expectations. The front-line is the bottom line: The employees in front of the customer are the ones they see. Look after them, teach them well, support them. Every face to face interaction is a moment of truth. If a customer interacts with 50 Cast Members (= employees) per day there are 50 moments of truth. If there are 49 great moments and 1 bad, which do you think the customer will remember? We need all moments of truth to be great. You have two ears, two eyes and one mouth, use them in that ratio: Listen to your customers, they are trying to tell you something. It is only when they have told you what they want that you can give them the help they need".

Google
"Focus on the user and all else will follow: Since the beginning, we've focused on providing the best user experience possible. Whether we're designing a new Internet browser or a new tweak to the look of the homepage, we take great care to ensure that they will ultimately serve you, rather than our

own internal goal or bottom line. Our homepage interface is clear and simple, and pages load instantly. Placement in search results is never sold to anyone, and advertising is not only clearly marked as such, it offers relevant content and is not distracting. And when we build new tools and applications, we believe they should work so well you don't have to consider how they might have been designed differently".

Amazon

"Our mission is to be Earth's most customer-centric company, where customers can find and discover anything they might want to buy online. We endeavor to offer our customers the lowest possible prices. Amazon has teams across the world working on behalf of its customers at Fulfillment Centers, which provide fast, reliable shipping directly from Amazon's retail websites, and Customer Service Centers, which provide 24/7 support. Our leaders start with the customer and work backwards. They work vigorously to earn and keep customer trust. Although leaders pay attention to competitors, they obsess over customers."

Apple

"We are at our best when we deliver enriching experiences. What we tell our staff: Approach customers with a personalized, warm welcome: Make sure customers are greeted by a friendly smile, Probe politely to understand the customer's needs (ask closed and open-ended questions), Present a solution for the customer to take home today, Listen for and resolve any issues or concerns: By truly listening and acknowledging the needs of your customers, you make your business an oasis of encouragement, empowerment, and excitement. End with a fond farewell and an invitation to return: There is a direct correlation between how people feel when they leave your business and how likely they are to return or recommend the experience to someone else".

Ultimately, delivering in excellence consistently, frequently, repetitively and easily will drive your dream clients to purchase your product or service without second-guessing. Customers expect consistent exceptional experiences across a diverse set of channels. And when the experience is not consistent from one channel to the next, it feels off. If you create the experience, they will bring in the income. Build a business or brand that makes you unforgettable so that you can gain loyal customers, build brand fans, and make more cash.

If you simply take the effort to improve yourself, your delivery will be powerful and your impact will be unforgettable.

@iamtaylorsimon #Captivate

Think
BIGGER

BOLDER

Braver!

SECRET
Strategy
#3

#3

How to Become a
Social Media Rockstar

"Visual marketing does not just sell a product or service - it sells an experience around your business." – Rebekah Radice

Through various social media outlets, the world is at your fingertips. It's never been more important to take advantage of social media platforms to capture your audience's attention with high-quality visual content. This secret will dive into the effectiveness of utilizing social media to connect and engage your audience with photos, videos, images, and infographics. This secret will also help you to use strategic tips and methods that will better position you to meet your business goals and reach your target audience. Statistics shows that the brain processes visual information 60,000 times faster than text. Social media is one of the most innovative communication tools that provide effective and cost-efficient marketing. If you don't have a lavish budget to use for marketing, don't fret. Social media is accessible to startup companies, solo-prenuers, and large organizations. Without a doubt, social media is a powerful tool that will help you achieve your dreams and attract your dream clients.

"If you want engagement, be engaging. Be conversational. Ask questions. Leave room for your audience to add their voice."
-Darren Rowse

Captivate on Facebook

➤ Public figures do not have private pages. If you are a pub   lic figure, set up a "fan" page. Personal Facebook pages are used for just that. Personal usage.

➤ If you want to use your Facebook page primarily for business, set up a "fan" page that is specifically designed and formatted for businesses.

➤ Create content that generates a conversation. You don't always have to post generic marketing content.

Get versatile by posting or reposting funny images and videos, questions, memes, blog posts, and surveys. Yes, it is important to post content that is related to your brand, but it is also beneficial to post or repost content unrelated to your business to open more conversation for your fans. Don't get too carried away by posting random content all the time. However, strategically identify other topics that your audience is passionate about and use that to engage them

➢ Both photos and videos are great for creating interaction with your fans on Facebook

➢ Integrate regular marketing methods in Facebook, but don't be afraid to change things up every now and then. Show behind the scene shots, do interviews, and have live webinars with special guests.

➢ Facebook live is an effective way to build your brand, captivate your audience, and drive them to your website, product, or service. I would recommend doing a Facebook live either once a day or twice a week depending on your level of comfortability. Long videos are great and will always draw a crowd, but make sure you are prepared to provide valuable content. Before getting on Facebook live, create an outline with 3 points and prepare a call to action to drive sales. If you are doing a 2-3 minute video, share your call to action or "Impossible to Resist" Freebie to convert them into paying customers!

➤ Give your audience the inside scoop to irresistible discounts and giveaways!

➤ The most appealing updates are ones that offer something. But don't give them everything; provide a clickable link that will direct them to where you want them to go.

➤ If you are going to provide a link, use https://bitly.com/ so that you can collect insights and track how many people are coming from Facebook.

➤ Engage with your followers by monitoring and managing comments, responses, and questions.

Captivate on Twitter

➤ Develop your voice and engage your audience with several passion points that fit your brand messaging.

➤ Images and videos add interest to your posts.

➤ People come to Twitter to have fun, so relax and captivate with intriguing posts.

➤ Stay fresh and up to date by posting frequently.

➤ Optimize your photos to fit the frame.

➢ Make mentions and share with short links like https://bitly.com/

➢ Use calls to action and invite people to retweet.

➢ Generate a conversation by retweeting your followers. Find out what they are interested in and they will be more interested in you.

➢ Use links to your website, blog, videos, or images.

➢ Edit your profile content and make it relevant to who you are and what your brand represents.

Captivate on Instagram

➢ Instagram is an image based social media platform

➢ Focus more on the solutions you provide and not the products you sale.

➢ Design and lifestyle are integrated in the Instagram platform, so think about how your product or service works in people's lives

➢ If your business is service-based, focus on the process behind the services that you provide. Share tips, quotes, and how-to's. Show your company culture and share your mission.

➢ Have Tip Tuesday, Motivational Monday, and use trending themes such as #tbt or Throw Back Thursday to increase engagement.

➢ Use filters, text, and stickers on the go.

➢ Popular brands on Instagram use their creativity to build a large community

➢ Instagram should not be used to commercialize your brand, but to stylize your brand and shows your brands personality.

➢ Post at least 3 times a day on Instagram, once in the morning, then in the afternoon, then late at night between 6:00pm-9:00pm.

➢ When people post comments, make sure you are monitoring their feedback and join in on the discussion or questions to interact with your fans.

➢ Use unique #hashtags that are promotion and campaign specific or popular #hashtags to increase likability and discoverability. Set up your main company/business #hashtag as well so that it makes it easier for people to find content related to your primary account. Use #hashtags sparingly and wisely so that you do not create confusion to your brand messaging.

➢ Build anticipation and offer exclusivity.

➢ Instagram only gives you one chance to apply a link to your profile. Never change your bio link again with https://linktr.ee/. This free app allows you to have one link that takes you to multiple destinations.

➢ If you are a business owner, create a business profile not a personal Instagram profile. Doing this will unlock extensive insights, analytics, and paid advertising.

➢ Use the new feature Instagram stories to capture behind-the-scene content. Experiment with Boomerang, short video clips, photos, and live video.

➢ In your bio, focus on your most important things: an event, product launch, promotion, or webinar.

➢ Placing the primary subject of your photos in only two thirds of the screen makes it more attractive to the eye.

Captivate on Google+

➢ You cannot use Google+ without a Google account.

➢ Post regularly and stay active. Doing this will boost you up Google's search engine. Remember, the higher you go, the more your audience will grow.

➢ Engage communities by taking advantage of the Circles feature and share different types of content that are relevant to different people.

➤ Share images, videos, and long posts.

➤ Use keywords in your about page to drive SEO.

Captivate on Linkdin

➤ Formal platform mainly for business professionals.

➤ Company pages support brand recognition

➤ Apply new skills and get endorsements to boost your credibility and impress potential clients.

➤ Link your website to drive traffic.

➤ Complete your profile 100%

➤ Post relevant content regularly

➤ Customize your Linkdin URL to make it easier for people to find you.

➤ First impressions matter when it comes to business matters. Having a professional headshot will appeal to your industry and peers.

➤ Make your resume experience more interesting with

video clips, PowerPoint slides, blogs, testimonials, and relevant quotes.

➢ Use job titles that makes you stand out.

➢ The best times to post on Linkdin are between 7am-9am

➢ Send a thank you message when people endorse you. This builds connection.

➢ Optimize your profile by adding a background banner.

Captivate on Pinterest

➢ Create a business account or convert your personal profile into a business account

➢ Make Pinterest boards that are relevant to your audience

➢ Use a lot of color, get playful, have fun. Make it beautiful and visual. The more captivating your content, the more engagement you will get.

➢ Boost traffic to your Pinterest by sharing your pins on all social media platforms.

➢ Create inspiration collages

➤ Use infographics, checklists, tutorials, quotes, videos

➤ Place company logo on images.

➤ Include a call to action to your pins.

Captivate on Periscope

➤ Use your platform as if it were a webinar or live training. You can limit the amount of replays so that you can increase retention and exclusivity.

➤ Utilize the content that you get from Periscope and repurpose it for Facebook, Youtube, and blogs.

➤ Stay consistent by announcing a particular day that you will do your Periscopes. For instance, you can plan to do a Periscope on Tuesdays and Thursdays evenings at 6pm. Make sure you show up because your viewers will be waiting for you!

➤ Share your live speaking with your online audience and invite them to get involved.

➤ Announce deals, promote your book, and advertise your business.

➤ Leverage behind the scene moments to attract your

audience.

ON BRAND SOCIAL MEDIA

Let's start with the basics. Every social media platform should be <u>on brand.</u> The goal of your profiles is to get people to pay attention to you and your social media activities. Essentially, this section explains how to become more consistent on your social media accounts.

1. Stick with One Picture
Remember, consistency is key. If different companies used different logos in different places, mass confusion would reign. Your avatar is your social-media logo, so use the same one everywhere. An avatar is the small image that everyone is able to see first before making the decision to browse around. It validates who you or your business is so that people can identify which business or brand you are. Most importantly, it supports the narrative that you are likable, trustworthy, and competent. Your brand avatar should not show your family, friends, dog, or car. This also means, do not use a logo or graphic design unless your avatar is for your business or an organization. This will promote brand recognition on your social-media platforms and reduce any questions.

2. Screen Names
Pick a neutral screen name on all platforms (Not @ taycute4u). By the way, this used to be my old social media handle. Clever right? Okay, maybe not so much. Today's witty name could be tomorrow's regret. Poten-

tial employers, universities, and in this case, clients are looking for you. It's not the place for complexity, confusion, or childhood nicknames. Make it easy for people to find you. And of course, keep it professional because you never know who is watching you. For example, @iamtaylorsimon is on Instagram and @iamtaylorsimon is on Twitter. If you're not able to have the same exact name for each platform, use the closest name possible. In my case, if @iamtaylorsimon were not available for Google+, then I would choose +TaylorSimon.

3. Master your Mantra and Express your Tagline

Most profiles allow you to add a tagline to your profile. Make this at least two to four words that explain why you or your organization exists and apply it to any area provided to place relevant biographical text. For the sake of consistency, make sure that your tagline/mantra is the same on every platform. Here are a few examples of effective mantras and taglines for well-known companies:

- Nike: just do it
- Apple: think different
- Google: democratizing information
- Facebook: move fast with infrastructure

4. Banners and Covers

Social media platforms allow a second, larger photo, called a "cover" (Google+, Facebook, and LinkedIn) or "header" (Twitter). This area is a place where you can expand your brand value or damage your social media credibility. Make sure that you change the default design that each platform provides. If you don't add a custom photo, you are screaming that you are clueless about social media. With your cover photo, it is important to keep this image consistent on each platform. Each platform has different optimal dimensions of cover/header photos.

Here are the appropriate files sizes for your profile picture and cover/header photos:

Facebook
Cover photo 851 x 315 pixels
Avatar size upload 180 x 180 pixels, preview 160 x 160 pixels

Instagram
Profile photo 180 x 180 pixels

Twitter
Header image 1,500 x 500 pixels
Background 1280 x 1024 pixels
Profile photo 400 x 400 pixels

Youtube
Channel art 2,560 x 1,440 pixels
Channel icon 800 x 800 pixels

Pinterest
Profile image 165 x 165 pixels
Board cover image 22 x 150 pixels

LinkedIn Company Profile

LinkedIn cover photo 974 x 300 pixels
LinkedIn logo 100 x 60 pixels
LinkedIn personal profile avatar 500 x 500 pixels
Background photo for premium users (rolling out to everyone) between 1,000 X 425 and 4,000 X 4,000 pixels

5. Brand Color Consistency

Apply your specific brand colors to increase brand awareness and recognition. If your logo icon is white and one of your brand colors is blue, place your white logo on top of the blue background.

6. Crisp and Clickable

Make sure the images that you use for your avatar and cover are big and crisp when people click on it. Upload a picture for your avatar that is at least 600 pixels wide.

"The key to engaging content?
Think bigger, bolder and braver."

-Anna Handley

People like People

& If You
Like People

People will like
YOU!

SECRET
Strategy
#4

#4

Master Your Charm

Creating an irresistible brand takes becoming an irresistible person. In the same way, great leaders are good communicators. If you want to be in the lead, start making some noise and letting your voice be heard. This means becoming more visible, attending business networking events or seminars, and flooding the timelines of your fans with interesting periscopes, videos, and posts. Developing a daily habit of getting involved at any capacity can help anyone master his or her charm and increase brand visibility.

Showing up and showing value will enlighten your fans. It let's them know that you care enough to give them what they want, which is to see your lovely face and hear from the expert you were born to be. **Yes, the people want to see you.** And when I mean people, I mean your dream clients. Honestly, people don't want to do business with a product, they want to do business with a person. When a human being is not visible, some people tend to lose trust and may think you're a robot or something. <u>You don't want that.</u> That may be a little far-fetched, but it's true. Our world is emotionally driven, which means that a person (you), must evoke that emotion by sharing a captivating story, posting sharable pictures, engaging with followers, and being interesting. This secret is about harnessing the power of personality and getting people to love you.

AWKWARD SUSIE AND BORING BOB

Awkward Susie

No one wants to do business with *Awkward Susie*. Who's Awkward Susie? Awkward Susie is the lady who attends networking events only to awkwardly stand in the corner with a glass of pineapple juice in her hand. She's that person that hates going to events, but only attends them because she's currently in a financial deficit and needs to make money fast. Susie wears her nametag but no one knows her name because she only talks to people that she knows. When she does speak, weird eye contact and frequent awkward pauses arise.

She has trouble with making meaningful connections. Instead of being social, she would rather be at home in her pjs watching repeat episodes of Judge Judy. Anything outside of Susie's comfort zone makes her shut down and causes her palms to sweat. But, she's up for small talk just to keep the lights on.

Let's not forget she showed up late. Finally, someone walks up to her with a warm smile to introduce themself. The conversation goes well and truth be told, Susie actually has a great product. When they try to exchange cards, Susie looks in her purse only to find out that she ran out of business cards. **Awkward.**

Luckily, her new connection receives Susie's alternative suggestion to tare off a ridged sheet of tablet paper to write her contact information down.

Awkward.

Intrigued by Susie's product, this new potential client and connection searches for Susie on Facebook. This potential client was led only to find a private page with Susie's business name with no avatar picture, and very little engagement. Actually, the last time she was on social media was about a year ago. Awkward.

Boring Bob

Then there is *Boring Bob*.
Boring kills sales.
Boring kills deals.
Boring kills networking events.
Boring kills relationships. And yes, you've guessed it.
Boring kills dates.

Boring has mastered the concept of same. To Boring, same is safe. He is consistent with doing the same old thing all the time. Now, I'm not talking about the consistency that I mentioned in the previous chapter. Boring Bob is consistent at doing nothing. No innovation. No new systems. No strategy. No branding. No marketing. No connections. No real change. Just boring. He honestly thinks he doesn't need all of that. Responsive website maybe. Social media presence not so much. Marketing – He'll take some business cards. Boring Bob is okay with doing only what he is familiar with. He's comfortable with same. He would rather not stand out and settles for doing just enough to get by. What worked 20 years ago, works well for him now.

Tell him something that he doesn't know and he will tell you what you don't know. Instead of listening to the expert, he thinks he is an expert at everything. In addition, he would rather scroll on social media and scoff at the amazing things that are happening in other people's lives than actually implement strategy that will elevate his own business and lifestyle. He is a great retainer of information. Retained and never released.

Boring Bob does not attend networking events because he honestly does not like people. People make him nervous so he would rather stay at home and chill. Boring Bob wants to be successful, but does not put in the work to achieve it. He's cool with boring. Boring Bob hates taking risks and see things only from his perspective. It's his way or the highway. His experience is enough exposure. Boring Bob will only share what he wants you to hear and is not comfortable will being personable.

"Relatability stinks," says Boring Bob. Boring has no interest in upgrading his wardrobe. He's cool with Dickies and a crisp, starched button down white shirt with patent leather shoes. Boring Bob doesn't like a whole lot of commotion. He's good with quiet. His life's mantra is "Keep it Stupid Simple". Which means go to work, pay the bills, go home, take a bath, eat, go to sleep. Repeat. Boring Bob is comfortable with being a regular average Joe. *Less stress. Less success. Nothing more. Nothing less.*

Perfect is Boring

@iamtaylorsimon #Captivate

Question:

Who would you identify yourself as? Awkward Susie or Boring Bob? Or are you both?

The Harsh Reality

The truth is, there is some point in everyone's life where we become Awkward Susie or Boring Bob. So don't feel bad. But let's face it, when we allow ourselves to take on either identity, we take on the unfriendly consequences that tag along with them. Being boring can be a benefit for some, but in the case of mastering your charm, boring is bad. Some may even call awkward cute, but it can cut into considerable opportunities.

7 STEPS TO MASTERING YOUR CHARM

It's not enough to just do your work and expect the wealth to flow in. Today, you must be charming, likable, magnetic, and have impressive influence. Which means, people must like you. Yes, you cannot captivate your dream clients if they do not consider you as likeable. Charm gets you places, attracts people, and brings in the profits. It is a powerful quality that makes people love you. Charisma will open doors for you that you would never imagine.

It will get you that one huge contract you've been waiting for. It will place you in the presence of prestigious people. It will unlock that financial breakthrough you've been praying for. It will end the misery of living in a mystery. Charm is about being infectious.

It's about loving yourself when no one likes you.

It's about showing up when no one is listening and believing that they will come. It's about stepping out, standing out, and sitting tall in the midst of those who are doing the same thing as you. Confidence is magnetic. Charm is magnetic. Charming people are always ready. Charming people are able to attract and engage people.

Now I'm not talking about the type of mumbo jumbo charm. Nor am I speaking of charm that activates delusion, confusion, and manipulation. I'm speaking about the charm that wins hearts. Charm that gives choice and not control. Yes, the type of charm that sustains stability in your business or your brand. That charm comes from you, simply being….YOU.

Get ready to radiate warmth that will draw people to you through seven steps that will help you charm the dream client that you have been trying to win over for years.

Knowing your audience is the cornerstone of captivation.

@iamtaylorsimon #Captivate

Enrich your Insight

To charm your audience is to know your audience. Knowing your audience is the cornerstone of captivation. Enriching your insight will help you to identify their needs. Yes, this means that you will have to do your research. Understanding the needs and desires of your dream client will aid in tailoring a message or product that speaks specifically to them. Do your research and decode your audience's calling, concerns, and cares. This method will help you to determine what they are called to do, their greatest pain points, fears, deepest desires, and dreams.

This is not the time for imputing what you "think" you know about your client. Instead, this is about backing up your knowledge with marketable data and analytics. There is nothing more horrid than having a conversation with someone and automatically assuming that they are one way, when they are not. This creates an "Awkward Susie" moment and you want to prevent that from happening. If you really want to impress your audience with charm, start by doing some research and deliver a package that is Taylor Made just for them. Trust me, they are going to love it!

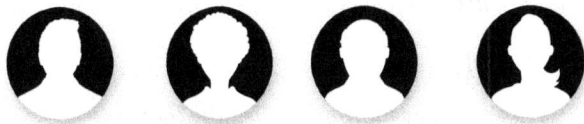

Collecting market research will help you to create your dream client avatar or persona. Your dream client avatar is an individual with a face, name, personality, specific demographic and other distinctive characteristics. Ultimately, your client avatar is a reflection of who you believe you are called to serve. Identifying whom you are called to serve will help you to develop a clear persona of your client avatar.

Create a Customer
Who Creates Customers
@iamtaylorsimon #Captivate

To help you to get started on creating your dream client avatar, here are a few key questions to ask yourself:

- *What age group are they? Millennials? Gen X? Baby Boomers?*
- *Are they male or female, or both?*
- *Do they live in the city, suburbs, or rural areas?*
- *Where do they like to shop? Online shoppers? Target or Nordstrom's?*
- *What religion is my dream client? Does it matter? What are their beliefs?*
- *What is their culture? Where are they from?*
- *Are they college educated or do they just have a high school diploma?*
- *Are they single moms? Single dads?*
- *Do they maintain a healthy lifestyle?*
- *Are they middle class or upper class?*
- *Are they empty nesters?*
- *What drives them?*
- *What do they aspire to be?*
- *What language do they use? Emojis?*
- *What do they like to do in their free time?*
- *What publications do they like to read? Sources of information they refer to?*
- *Do they have children? If so, how many, and why does this matter?*
- *Are they married or single?*
- *Where are they hanging out?*
- *Do they have children? If so, how many?*
- *What are their challenges? Pain points? What makes them*

tick?
- *What are their strengths? Weaknesses?*
- *What are their goals and values?*

With these questions, you will be ready to tackle the crowd with confidence and laser sharp focus. No more bumping into shoulders, because your eyes are on the people you are equipped to serve the most. Collecting this information will definitely charm your client because you know who they are and where they are. Everything must be specific, focused, and precise. Wouldn't it be super impressive if someone walked into your office desiring to work with you and knew everything about you because they are truly interested in serving you to the best of their abilities? Without question, they may get some cool points with the potential of getting hired for the job.

Your avatar needs to speak to your ideal customer in a way that when they go to your website, it's almost like you've read their mind. There are major benefits to this mad method, so don't get overwhelmed by the amount of information. Understanding their struggles, pain points, or frustrations will help you to create solutions and marketable messages that address their problems. Developing new products, services, or copy that caters to their needs will charm your ideal client to take action. Remember, copy that connects will stick!

Here are some examples on how you can start your messaging:

Are you tired of feeling overwhelmed with…?
Have you ever wanted to go on paid international vacations…?
Want laptop free weeknights with your wife…?

These are just a few examples out of many. If the answers to your questions are not yes every time, then back to the drawing board you go. Your dream client should be able to answer your questions with a "YES… YES!" response. Your yes will heighten your chances of building trust, authority, and credibility. Understanding the sources of information that they refer to will help you to determine where to advertise and market your brand.

Marketing at the right place, at the right time, to the right people will manifest miraculous results.

@iamtaylorsimon #Captivate

Detailed data will definitely help you to develop a strong client avatar story. Write their compelling storyline, share their most unspeakable thoughts, and watch your dream clients swarm in.

Example:
Chipotle

Mexican burrito chain Chipotle's branding and marketing strategy is completely focused on resonating with their primary customer avatar – millennials who care about the origin of their food.

With the tagline "Food With Integrity", Chipotle only uses sustainably raised ingredients from family farmers and when possible, organic and local produce. Meat comes from animals raised humanely and without the use of antibiotics or added hormones.

Chipotle gained extra reputation by shying away from traditional media because millennials felt the format was inauthentic and difficult to connect with.

Step aside, fast food, Chipotle's here to Taco – ver.

Entice your Audience

To entice your audience, you must have an impeccable product, a dynamic presentation, exceptional designs, contagious content, and an approachable appearance. Everything that represents you should look, feel, and if applicable, sound and smell amazing. This also means, creating a great user interface on your website. Charm begins with physical attraction. It starts with what people are able to see. What they see will determine what they will do. This means to package your product so well that they will have no choice but to take a second glance. Make them fall in love with your brand by simply smiling. Looking like the Grinch Who Stole Christmas all the time does not draw people to you. It makes them run away. But smiling creates a sensory connection that makes people feel comfortable enough to approach you. Have you ever smiled at someone and they didn't smile back? Well, it either means that you have something in your teeth, or their just not fit to be your ideal client.

You will have those occasional clients who ignore the bells and whistles. But don't let that keep you from smiling because it's not about charming any client, its about attracting the right client. What if you don't feel like smiling? If smiling isn't your thing anymore, I encourage you to restore that beautiful smile of yours by thinking about if what you are doing is what you are supposed to be doing. If you are truly passionate about what you do, smiling should become second nature. Increase your passion level by revisiting your dream and ditching what seems like a drab job.

Enticing your audience is about having brand bait. An ethical one of course. Specifically, a free giveaway that you can use to make your brand magnetic. This could include a free eBook, email series, webinar, worksheets, chapter of your first book or more. People love free stuff, plain and simple. But free becomes more effective when you have something that they actually want.

Engage your Audience

*Engage with intention,
persuade with passion and persistence.*

@iamtaylorsimon #Captivate

When you are engaging your clients, drive them with your passion and empower them with incredible content. Show them that you truly care and want them to succeed as much as you want to succeed. Engagement is not about you. It's about the people and how you can get them to interact with what you have to offer them. Show them your truth and charm them with imperfection. Open up and radiate with relatability to win hearts.

People love authentic people. Nowadays, most people can sense if someone is being fake or not. This means that your strategy should reveal authenticity. Real talk. Real life. With real people. Point Blank Period.

If you want to engage your dream clients you must make the intentional effort to be seen and heard. They cannot see you with your head down. Pick your head up and show the world what you are capable of by getting involved and getting active through multiple outlets. Dreamer, your presence is powerful and once you allow people to see that, the charm is on. Engaging your audience requires consistent avatar interaction. Interaction with your target audience creates instant attraction and drives them to become apart of your tribe or community.

Social media is an effective platform that allows you to engage your target audience. Facebook and Periscope offers easy video features that allow you to go live in real time or in no time. Creating videos live or pre-recorded helps you to increase visibility and brand exposure. Using the live features will position you as an expert. Why? Because you will be available and accessible to answer any of your audience's questions that will eventually charm them with your expertise. You literally become the hero of the hour. Become the life of the party with a content strategy that appeals to your audiences' emotions.

Going over board with promotional posts can give your audience the impression that a sale is more important that a soul. This behavior is almost equivalent to the annoying person at the networking event who dominates the conversation bragging about his or her accomplishments.

There is a time for social proof and a time for social growth.

@iamtaylorsimon #Captivate

Defining the two before delivering your content will help you to create a healthy balance of content distribution to bring in the funds and the brand fans! Creating content that is strong, conversational, and evokes emotion will build stronger engagement and audience growth. People are more likely to retweet, repost, share, or comment when your content activates their imagination and speaks directly to their heart. *Remember, you're marketing to humans, not robots.* Humans respond to a person, so make things personable.

Another easy way to engage your audience and attract social following is to offer your customers incentives to "like", follow, or connect with your business. Hosting a contest can generate valuable buzz about your business, create brand affinity and captivate potential customers to check out your website. Free giveaways are an excellent way to generate leads and build your email list. Although not all participants will convert to a loyal client, at least they can say that they've had an encounter with you. Most charming one, using this strategy will give you the ability to nurture your dream clients into being paid clients through worthwhile experiences.

Enlighten with Information

Enlighten your audience with information by inventing authentic ideas and sticking with your powerful message. If you are in the coaching industry, and you specialize in business coaching, there are probably zillions of other business coaches recycling the same exact information. I've even asked myself "why bother when there are a bajillion other talented creatives out there"?

Everyone is coaching. Everyone is hustling.

Honestly, it can get a bit discouraging when you see someone else doing the same thing you're doing. And it can get even more awkward when it "seems" like they're doing it better then you. Dreamer, don't get intimidated by others doing the same thing as you. There is enough room for everyone to be successful. And guess what? No one can do it like you. When you fall into the comparison trap, you will begin to fall like quicksand and lose the desire to hustle and create. When you're doing what you love to do and give your best while doing it, that draws the masses.

Think about Beyoncé. She sings and performs, knowing that there are tons of other talented and gifted performers and singers who are doing the same thing as her. But does that stop her? Of course not. Her unique audience loves her for being her and delivering the best performances. There are zillions of other performers that may even look better and sing better than her. But no one sings like Beyoncé. No one delivers like Beyoncé. No one sounds like Beyoncé.

This is equivalent to your business. The information that you have to share may be the same, but your sound is different, your approach is unique, and your perspective is outstanding. That's charming. Have you heard of the phrase, "don't reinvent the wheel"? Well don't. This world is filled with recycled information that you were meant to use to refuel them with in a unique way. The second part of this quote says, "realign it". Which means to just work on making it better then anyone else. Now I'm not saying that you cannot reinvent the wheel, I'm just sharing a more effective route that will keep you from wasting time trying to create new information or develop products or systems that have already been done before you.

Instead of repeating the information, improve the information and add your special touch to it. Sometimes it's not about what you say or put out there, it's about how you say it and the testimony given that supports it. Everyone may be sharing the same message, but you have a different story. In the midst of duplicated information, yours reign supreme.

Another tip when enlightening your audience with information is to not always assume that people know what you're talking about before you talk about it. Doing this completely diminishes your creative flow. The first time they heard it, they probably didn't get it, but when you enlightened them with your information it sticks. Although the material is the same, the methods in which it is used have changed. You have the ability to provide your ideal clients an entirely new perspective or approach to receiving and handling the information, concept, or system.

Eliminate the Fear

Charming people are fearless. They are not without fear, but take a chance through the fear. They look fear in the face and do it anyway. Have you ever wanted to go to the gym, but decided not to because of the excuse or reasoning of it being too crowded? Although this seems like a fair excuse, it's not really an excuse at all, it's fear. Fear of people. Imagine doing the things that you know that you are called to do. Things that make you happy, give you a sense of fulfillment, and makes your life better. But often times, we don't do it because we are afraid of people. Afraid of what people might think, afraid of being criticized, afraid of being accepted, afraid of being embarrassed, afraid of success, afraid of failure, or afraid of being hurt by people.

I was afraid of writing this book. I was afraid that it wouldn't be good enough, afraid that I wouldn't get good ratings, or afraid of the potential success that it might bring. There have been plenty of times where I allowed fear to dictate my progress and performance in business. Fear kept me from doing a lot of things, going a lot of places, and meeting a lot of people. Just like the excuse for not going to the gym, I used to come up with excuses and reasoning to justify my behavior. It's funny how a simple excuse can blind us from seeing the fear that truly lies dormant within us.

To be charming, you must eliminate the fear that is holding you back. Fear will keep you from letting go of the remote control and going to that networking event. It will push you in the corner, just to prevent you from connecting with someone new to get your next big deal. It will keep you with your face in your phone rather than being engaged with people around you. Fear will hinder you from following up and following through. Fear will keep you from doing things that benefit others. Fear will hold you hostage to past hurt. Fear will keep you from going live on social media. Fear will keep you from making that call or sending that email. Fear's job is to keep you from launching your witty invention, resourceful program, or amazing project. It will also keep you from going to the gym to get in shape.

I have heard so many people, including myself, say, "I don't like people". But in all actuality, it's no longer "I don't like people", it's really "I fear people". We are all in the business of people because people purchase the products. So how can we not "like" people, when people are the ones that are used as a source of income and increase? At this moment, I challenge you to let go of any pre-conceived notion about people and go to the people. Go to the people that need your service or product and they will gravitate to you.

Understand that by knowing your ideal client, you can approach them courageously and without fear. Feel the fear and follow through no matter what. Identify that people need you. People need what you have and want to hear what you have to say regardless if they want to or not. Know that what you have to offer is important and valuable. If you don't believe in you, how can you expect anyone else to believe in you? Have you ever listened to yourself talk about your business? Record yourself saying your 30-45 second elevator speech and listen for enthusiasm. If you were your dream client listening to that recording, would you say that the person is passionate or timid? When you say your elevator speech aloud, say it with expectation. Say it expecting that people are actively listening and actively buying your services or products because fear has lost its grip. Overcome your fear of people so that you can become more effective in charming your way into your next big break.

Fear is Afraid of You

@iamtaylorsimon #Captivate

Expand your Influence with Innovation

Expanding your circle of influence calls for embracing innovation. Innovation requires looking beyond what is right in front of you and adopting new methods and trends. Expanding influence is not something that happens to people who sit still. Your influence cannot change if you remain in the same patterns and habits that you currently have, or surround yourself with the same people. Being deliberate and proactive about trying new things, forming new connections, and meeting new people are all ways to become more influential. Asking yourself the right questions will bring about innovation. *Don't ask why something is happening; ask how you can make it better.* Instead of harboring over the problem, develop a solution and focus on the possibilities. Remain optimistic and always look for fresh insight and ideas that will elevate your business or brand.

Here are some questions that you can ask yourself to stir innovation and increase influence:

How can I leave this situation better than I found it?
How can I meet and get to know new people?
How can I help and inspire the people around me?
How can I be a solution in this situation?
How can I make myself available to serve?
How can I bring about change into my organization, business, or brand?
How can I not only make a difference, but be a difference?

Mastering your craft is essential when expanding your influence through innovation. This means that you are constantly working on your skill set. Influential people are not mediocre. After you have obtained some level of maturity or mastery in an area, growth does not stop there. Reading books, attending events or webinars, having a mentor, doing research, and trying new things, can develop your skill set.

Execute in Excellence

Charming people execute in excellence. They show up and stay ready. When you have mastered the art of charm, you don't wait for someone to make a move because you make the move first. If you started your first webinar only to deliver to an audience of 2 people, show up in excellence and give value as if it was 2000 people. Holding nothing back, giving it all that you've got. Charming people don't wait for the people to come, they show up and the people follow.

Don't leave anything behind. That means your

business cards or any other promotional material. If you are attending a business networking event or going to Wal-Mart, always keep a couple of extra business cards in your wallet, your pocket, and a reasonable amount in the car. You never know who you may come across. For women, find a small pouch that perfectly fits your business cards so that you are staying organized and not having to dive into your purse to find them. Doing this wastes time and makes you look like Awkward Susie.

Consider every minute as your last moment to gain an opportunity that will change your life.

@iamtaylorsimon #Captivate

If you desire more income, your finances are on the line. If you want more family time, your family and children is on the line. If you desire happiness, your well-being is on the line. All of these things are depending on you to show up and put your best foot forward (without the patent leather shoes). Don't miss a minute to charm your client or you could miss a lifetime of fulfillment and enduring success. You have potential, now use these tips to become a pro at charming your dream clients.

Did you know?

Ecommerce sites with product pages optimized for mobile browsing saw:

o 30% Increase in sales
o 50% Decrease in bounce
o 70% Increase in product sold

People like people. And if you like people, people will like you.

@iamtaylorsimon #Captivate

CONVERSATION STARTERS FOR NETWORKING EVENTS

The first rule of networking: Ask answerable questions. The second rule: **Stop talking about yourself.** Here are a couple of conversation starters that you can use to increase your charm.

- Hi! I'm _____.
- Is this your first event?

- How did you hear about it?
- What made you come?
- Have you found it useful before?
- Do you know anyone else?
- Are you from _____?
- Few are really from here. Where did you move?
- What kind of business are you in?
- What do you do besides work?

The secret to networking is to be seen as a really interesting person. People remember you as interesting if you ask questions. Charming people don't share tons of information about themselves, they share tidbits to keep people hooked. People like to talk and tell you things, so let them. When you listen and let them be heard, you make them feel important and valued. Be the most interesting person in the room by finding out everything there is to know about another person. As you're talking with them, give eye contact, be enthusiastic, nod and give appropriate feedback and responses to their opinion. Most importantly, remember their name. When you remember people's name, they will make the effort to remember yours. This becomes a great benefit if you are interested in collaboration or taking them on as a client.

When you are done chatting with them, use some of the great information you just found out and introduce them to someone else. Don't forget to get their business card and write a little note about what you learned about them so you can remember it later.

You

won't have to

force opportunities

that are

meant for you...

SECRET
Strategy
#5

#5

Captivating Web Presence

"Packaging a powerful presence with polished pictures positions you for prolonged success and plenty profits".

@iamtaylorsimon #Captivate

Your website homepage is your business' virtual storefront. What is said and seen on the outside will determine whether or not people will make the decision to go in and browse for more information or make a purchase. Your homepage is also your website elevator speech. The content should be customer centric. But not just to any client, but your dream client.

Your homepage should be magnetic. Its purpose should drive visitors to take action. A great website experience begins with a dynamic webpage. If your website is just existing and not converting visitors into loyal paying clients, then your website is not fulfilling its true purpose.

When others see greatness,
they are drawn by greatness.

@iamtaylorsimon #Captivate

Keeping things consistent and less confusing will raise visitor retention and increase their attention span. A client-attractive homepage design with effective user experience is one of the most beneficial investments a brand can make. But if you've spent thousands of dollars on your website and it is not bringing the attention that you deserve, rethinking your strategy may not be such a bad idea. I could discuss the most effective and essential elements that are needed for the entire website, but I believe that starting with your homepage will help you make a greater impact. Why? Because your homepage is what determines your visitor's next step. So how do you create a captivating homepage presence that captures your clients and influences them to stick around? Ultimately, it's about providing great visual design, clear copy, efficient tech, and you.

Essential Elements of a Captivating Homepage Design

The 5 Second Rule. Recent studies have shown that you have just FIVE seconds to engage and influence a new visitor to stay on your website. They will judge your whole website (often unfairly) in those 5 seconds just from looking at your homepage – much in the same way that people judge a book by its cover in a matter of seconds. And if you don't captivate and engage them very well quickly, they often won't convert for your website goals (like orders or signups), or worst still, will leave your website immediately!

Honestly, no one likes slow loading web pages. Most people want things fast and if it does not catch their attention quick enough, they will move on the find the next big thing. That's where the 5-second rule comes in. If your homepage is dialing up like the classic Yahoo dial, you may not meet the 5-second rule.

Your visitors will lose patience and abandon your website to work with a competitor whose content loads much quicker. Even Google doesn't like slow webpages. Did you know that Google will penalize your website in their rankings if your homepage loads too slow? Simple things to speed up load times involve reducing image sizes and making your code more efficient.

A resource like tools.pingdom.com is a great tool that can check the speed of your website. You can also use a tool like YSlow to figure out certain elements that are slow loading that need optimizing.

Responsive Functionality Adopting innovative trends to meet the ever-changing standards of technology is essential for captivating your dream clients. With the growth of mobile devices, social media, tablets, and virtual gadgets it is essential that your website is compatible on all devices. Regardless of what device your dream client may be using, you want to make sure that your website is easily accessible and ready on the go.

Making your website responsive on both mobile and desktop devices invites your prospects to visit your website anytime, anywhere, in any form. According to statistics, more than 58% of American adults own a smart phone and almost 60% percent of traffic is from mobile devices. Going responsive places you in a pool of over 55% of social media consumption that now happens on mobile devices, sharing links from Facebook, YouTube, Twitter, or Google Plus. This means that even more traffic will be driven from mobile devices. Making responsive improvements on your website will help your site perform better Google search rankings.

There are plenty of business opportunities out there for you to take advantage of, but they go back to leveraging the power of responsive development. Improve your brand perception and boost your website conversions by implementing a responsive website.

Irresistible Freebies Let's face it. People love free stuff. Well at least I do! Whenever you put a dangling worm on a fishing line and drop it into the water, the fish will eventually come. In this case, whenever you give your dream clients what they want, they will come. I like to call this freebie your brand magnet.

Creating free "impossible to resist" content and providing easy access to them above the fold will activate the exchange. What's the exchange? The exchange is your valuable free bonus for their email address. When you have effectively positioned your valuable freebie, you grant yourself immediate access to their virtual world. Well, at least part of it.

It is said that 98% of people leave websites without converting. Don't freak out about the numbers! This just means that you have to go the extra mile to captivate them into that conversion. Most of the time, potential prospects are browsing and researching. Often times, your dream clients may be interested in your products or services but are not in the buying stage yet. How do you reel them back in? With your "impossible to resist" freebie to capture there email address and start building your email list. This list is a great way to further engage your dream clients, send personalized messages, and captivate them to return to your website and make a purchase.

I could go on and on about email lists, but for now, I just wanted to briefly touch this subject so that you have a basic understanding of the importance of building your email list. Nonetheless, your freebies accelerate the growth of your email list, boosts traffic to your website, and serves as a hook to get people interested in investing in your incredible services and products.

You won't have to force opportunities that are meant for you

@iamtaylorsimon #Captivate

List of 35 "Impossible to Resist" Freebies:

1. Create quote book
2. Audio Series/Pod Cast
3. DVD Series (physical CD's or link's)
4. Tele-Class
5. Interactive Checklist
6. Email Series
7. Free Guide
8. Webinar/Webinar Series
9. Free Events
10. Free Physical Books
11. Infographics
12. Printable
13. Text for a Free Gift using https://www.callloop.com/
14. Free Templates
15. Video Series
16. Free Ebook
17. Free Toolkits
18. Free Worksheets
19. Goal Sheets
20. A free report
21. Free Teleseminar
22. Mp3's
23. Free Workbooks
24. Free Graphics
25. Free Instrumentals
26. Free Membership
27. 7-Step Course
28. Free Recipe
29. Access to a contest
30. A Coupon of Discount Code
31. Free Consultation
32. Free Strategy Call

33. Free Tips or Tools
34. Access to exclusive/private FB group
35. Free Audits

There is no such thing as giving too much information, but there is a such thing as knowing when and how to distribute it.

@iamtaylorsimon #Captivate

Put your best stuff above the fold. Let's start with explaining what "the fold" is. Primarily, the fold is the content that is visible on your initial homepage load. It is the first thing that your visitors see on your page before scrolling down to browse for more. The fold is prime for immediate captivation. Positioning your most engaging client targeting content above the fold is key. Now this does not mean to overload them with tons of annoying pop-ups, distracting colors, or unnecessary images. Squeezing everything of importance at the top of your website will create overwhelm for your visitors.

Ultimately, the top of your website homepage is the spot where you reveal your Authority Banner, display your call to action, and post relevant images of a person or product. Connect your visitors with a familiar face or your most popular product. These elements are essential in creating something that I like to call your Authority Banner. Your Authority Banner is the banner that is above the fold primarily used to display a bold pose of yourself or your product, value proposition, and Power Statement visuals.

In marketing, your value proposition is a persuasive statement of why your prospects should do business with you and how your product or service will benefit and serve them. It clearly defines the core of your brilliant ideas that makes you the best in your industry, is consistent with your brand messaging, and specific in approach. It also provides the proof that you can deliver value. If you are going to say, "My pies are the best pies in the world" then you need proof.

Telling people what you are is simply not enough. They do not want to be coddled with clever slogans and catch phrases.

People need proof.

They want to believe you, but without proof, your efforts sound more like marketing chatter instead of marketing strategy. Being the best isn't enough, but showing value produces the best results. Therefore, you cannot have the what and the who, without the why. People may understand whom you are and what you have to offer, but if they do not know why they need to invest in you, your efforts become meaningless. Showing that you are worth it supports your value proposition. You can use methods such as case studies, testimonials, and common sense.

Other elements to further demonstrate a strong value prop are powerful statement visuals, an effective headline and sub-headline, a list of key benefits, and a call to action. You can also alternate bold and thin fonts to highlight trigger words that would attract your prospects attention. Your Authority Image could be a large pleasant, bold image of you posing with authority and exuding unfading confidence with an inviting facial expression.

If the image is you, give it all you've got, it will determine whether or not people will see you as THE expert. If you are displaying an image of your product, make sure that it is clear, crisp, and consistent. Additionally, displaying video footage in the Authority Banner area increases engagement.

All of these elements do not need to be above the fold at the same time. You have the option to create what works for you. However, it is important that you not neglect them on your homepage. People need to believe that you are the one before showing interest. Increasing believability demands credibility.

Show them what you've got. Support it with facts. Secure it with a promise. Serve it in excellence.

Remember:
Show it.
Support it.
Secure it.
Serve it.

Below I have provided you a few examples of effective value statements from some companies that you may have heard of. Observe the usage of their verbiage. Identify how you can implement the same methods in your business. Don't be afraid to copy genius. Don't use it word from word of course, but remake it. Take what's been made and make it your own so that you can start experiencing the difference.

- A headline
- A sub-headline
- A list of key benefits
- An image
- A call to action
- A free giveaway

Trello

Trello is the free, flexible, and visual way to organize anything with anyone.

Drop the lengthy email threads, out-of-date spreadsheets, no-longer-so-sticky notes, and clunky software for managing your projects. Trello lets you see everything about your project in a single glance.

Sign Up – It's Free.

Trello

What is the company selling? A tool that helps you visually organize anything.
What is the benefit of using it? You can remove a lot

of random ways to keep track of information and condense it all into one place.

Who is the target customer for this product or service? People who want to be more organized.

What makes the offering different from competitors? It takes tasks and info and makes it visual.

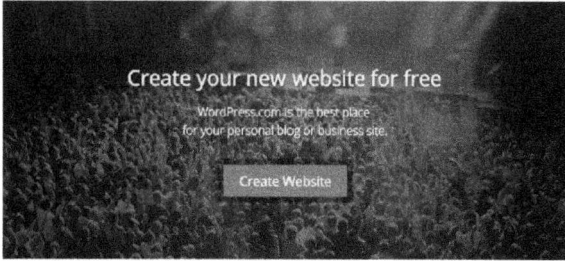

Wordpress

What is the company selling? A free website.

What is the benefit of using it? A free website.

Who is the target customer for this product or service? People who want a personal blog or a business site.

Captivating Touch: Clear call-to-action to create a website.

Navigate with Clarity and Confidence When guiding visitors through individual pages, you want to make sure that the directions are clear. Your website navigation bar is usually a collection of core links that are placed vertically to the left or horizontally near the top of the website page. Sometimes you will find a secondary navigation menu in the footer of the page. Visiting a website with disorganized menus is a hard route to follow. As a result, some tend to leave without question. Don't forget the 5 Second Rule!

According to Forrester Research
(http://www.usability.gov/)

- 50% of potential sales are lost because users can't find information
- 40% of users never return to a site when their first visit is a negative experience.

Before launching your site, double-check all links to ensure that they are being directed to the correct location. Doing this makes the process of viewing and exploring effortless. Navigation bars with clear and concise categories create fluid accessibility. In other words, long menu categories are not necessary.

Keep your categories short and simple. Everything should be easy to find, have meaning, and provide specific information. Superior navigation is a useful strategy to compliment your website design and increase page visits. Keep these tips in mind when developing your website!

If You Want a

PROMOTION

Dress like a

BOSS

SECRET
Strategy
#6

#6

Dress to Impress

Attracting your dream clients and maintaining cohesiveness in your brand requires extra care in your appearance. If you want to be a millionaire, you must carry yourself like a millionaire. Now I'm not saying that you have to avoid your budgets, overspend, and damage your financial goals. Splurging on material things to impress others is not the focus. In this case, I am more concerned with the minimum amount of attention that we give on our outer appearance when attempting to grow our business and elevate our lifestyle.

It's about looking like where you want to go and slaying every time anyone makes an acquaintance with you. It's about carrying a magnetic presence and exuding a power that is impossible to ignore. You are no longer selling the product or service because you have now become the product or service. To be the brand, you must wear the brand.

Branding goes beyond the storefront, services, products, website, and social media presence. Branding is an experience. In this experience, you must be willing expand and enhance your personal style and image for professional success.

If you simply take the time to improve yourself, your delivery will be powerful

@iamtaylorsimon #Captivate

Your wardrobe, personal hygiene, hairstyle, makeup, grooming, language, posture, and appearance matters in marketing your brand. At the same time, your personal appearance has a direct connection with professional service quality. Most people tend to assess the skill, quality, and value of your professional service based on your initial presentation. The quality of your appearance helps your potential clients in determining who you are, what you represent, and the credibility of your work.

In the same way, our brains are wired to look for social clues that tells us who people are, why they matter, and how they relate to us. Physical appearance is one of the most obvious clues that our brains look for when evaluating others.

For example, if you are a patient going to get a check up at the hospital and an individual with a white coat, stethoscope, well-groomed face and hair, and a bright smile walks in the room, you as the patient immediately identify the individual as a well-qualified, professional doctor. On the other hand, if you are in the hospital room and an individual with scruffy hair, blue jeans shorts, and a tank top enters the room with the same qualifications as the other doctor, you as the patient may get a little alarmed, feel uncomfortable, and politely (or angrily) ask for another doctor to assist you.

It is quite unfortunate that some people who are well qualified for a position doesn't get hired for the job due to their appearance. In the world that we live in, people disqualify the well qualified for their outer appearance instead of looking at the heart. This type of rejection is identified as discrimination and can cause much pain and strife.

Without a doubt, I absolutely disagree with this form of discrimination. There are so many people missing out on opportunities because of someone else's preconceived potential. But one thing that I have grown to understand is that even the person with the most potential can miss the mark when they neglect intentional and purposeful personal care.

Everyone has a talent, but not everyone has persistence. Anyone can have years of experience, but not everyone is willing to change. You may even have a gift, but not everyone has the determination to turn their gift into a valuable experience. What am I saying? You can have the passion, package, and potential, but if you are not persistent in your overall presentation you limit the possibility of achieving a lifetime of success. Yes, this means to love yourself and love what you do. Why? Because if you don't love yourself or what you do, it will show up in your image.

How you see yourself is a direct reflection of how you deliver your service.

@iamtaylorsimon #Captivate

Captivate with Confidence

You have to believe in you before anyone else believes in you. Your belief attracts what you see. If you believe that you are worthless, give no value, and have no potential, you will attract clients who see no value and treat your services and products as worthless. If you are constantly saying that you are broke, you will attract broke clients looking for a "hook up" or the "family discount". This is why confidence is key.

Confidence in who you are and what you have to offer can make anything look good. You can have on a plastic bag and people will be convinced that you are it! And if a plastic bag is all you've got, rock it to the best of your ability and sale it as if it were authentic piece of expensive couture.

Do what you can, with what you have, where you are

@iamtaylorsimon #Captivate

Dreamer, it does not matter how much money you have in the bank account, where you've been, or what you've done. The longevity of your success is dependent on the stability of your self-perception. How you perceive yourself, is exactly what others will perceive of you. You don't want people to have the wrong impression of who you are as the brand. You want to reflect and project the most authentic representation of who you are so that your dream clients are able to easily understand your brand messaging.

Don't let the voice of inferiority destroy your destiny. Tell the voice of insecurity, fear, and doubt to have a few seats so that you can be who you were created to be. You have a solution to someone else's problem. You are a problem-solver and a force to be reckoned with in your industry. If people don't know you yet, they will. If they don't know what you do yet, they will. The way to captivate people who don't believe in you is to captivate them with confidence. Sometimes wearing the nicest outfit cannot conceal lack of confidence. But in this chapter, I will teach you how to master your confidence, dress for success, and captivate your dream clients with a powerful and professional appearance.

YOUR SIGNATURE STYLE

Sharing your passion with others should become a

well-rounded experience from the time you walk into the door to the moment you leave the room. Attention to the smallest details creates the greatest results. Which means, what you wear and how you wear it is essential to creating an unforgettable experience. I am not saying to look like a corporate clone. Unless you work in a formal industry that requires you to wear a suit and tie, there is no reason to limit your options to express yourself. For instance, properly pressed jeans and a nice button down shirt may be appropriate for someone with a construction company. Whereas, a hair stylist may follow popular fashion trends to support the beauty industry. Wardrobe choices are important to showcasing your personal brand. You are the face of your brand and what you wear and how your wear it promotes it.

Generally, the best approach to expressing yourself in your business is to stay consistent with the theme of your brand. Sticking with the personality and theme of your personal brand everyday can become an extension of your larger brand. Remember, you are a walking brand. Getting creative in your personal style communicates your company values and helps you to find your target audience of like-minded dream clients. When you look the part, you get in the mindset for performing at a higher level. When you look good, you feel good and when you feel good, good things happen. Ultimately, the goal is to establish brand recognition and brand loyalty. Setting a standard for appearance and then supporting them with consistent wardrobe choices is a great way to achieve these goals.

Although consistency is key, sameness can be avoided. You don't have to wear the same thing everywhere in order to prove your point. However, you can wear statement pieces that people will remember you by. A good personal brand goes beyond the mundane, basic style choices, and instead creates a distinct look. You want to use your outfit to communicate what makes you and your business unique.

Consider wearing wardrobe pieces that are recognizable, versatile, unforgettable, and personifies a statement of identity. This type of branding strategy can consist of wearing a collection of bowties – colorful ones, solid ones, floral ones, and striped ones. Other examples can include funky socks, vibrant lipstick, flashy jewelry, hats, colorful handbags, patterned t-shirts, and glamorous glasses.

Another tip would be to coordinate with the colors of your brand. For instance, if your colors are orange, blue, and white, wear those colors to every function that requires you to put your business on blast. In the same way, if your brand theme is fun, energetic, and youthful, wear an outfit that supports and reemphasizes that theme.

The idea is to present yourself in a way that is impactful, authentic and memorable. A way that gets you noticed instantly. A way that will separate you from the crowd. A way that will captivate your dream clients. Through personal branding you will be able to give people a better understanding of who you are and what you do. When you remain consistent in your wardrobe, people associate you with qualities such as trustworthy, dependable, and charismatic. But when you settle for the sloppy look, people will associate you will qualities such as lazy, unreliable, and unprepared. Trust me, people will tell if you put effort in your business.

When you are constantly wearing something different, people will associate you with difference. Accessorizing serves as interesting conversation starters. I mean come on, who wouldn't want to talk to someone with colorful polka dot socks? There is so much power in personal branding through clothing and accessories. Your signature style should be planned, purposeful, and powerful. Don't be afraid to style for success. I guarantee you will manifest miracles in your business!

If you want a promotion, then dress like you're the boss

@iamtaylorsimon #Captivate

Savvy Style Tips

- Invest in an iron to keep clothes looking fresh
- For women, wear girdles or hosiery to create smooth lines. The idea is to achieve a more fashionable, cleaner look.
- Less clothes = Less reliable clients. Stay away from clothes that reveal too much skin. It will give off the wrong impression to your dream clients.
- Wear garments that are not too loose or too tight.
- Don't forget to style everything with a smile!
- There is beauty in balance.
- Don't overlook proper skin care
- It is better to be overdressed than underdressed. But before attending a networking event or speaking engagement, be sure to do your research on your audience prior to attending the event. Doing this will help you to captivate with strategy!
- For the guys, it is not appropriate to slab. Creating a more professional, sophisticated look requires a nice belt.

Hair Care

Every brand has a package and your hair care is apart of the package. No matter your occupation or industry, nicely groomed hair ties to your personal brand goals. As entrepreneurs and business leaders, just because some of us work at home, at a storefront or in an office doesn't mean that your hair should reflect that you don't care. In fact, if you look like you don't care, then people will perceive you as someone who does not care about their brand, or even worse, your potential client's brand.

Anywhere at all times should your hair reflect the excellence of your brand. Neat, well groomed, and tamed hair translates into a positive impression. Overlooking unintentional scruffy facial hair is overlooking the small details.

Eliminating the small unruly things can lead you to big unimaginable breakthroughs.

@iamtaylorsimon #Captivate

Although your hair care does not affect your ability to do a great job, your hairstyle does have an impact on your success. In the same way, keeping it tamed can influence your overall brand experience. Whether you like it or not, your hair gives off an impression and communicates a message. Just like your clothing, your hair has the ability to alter stereotypes. For example, if have dark brown hair with blue highlights, people can perceive you as a fun and vivacious. Depending on how you flaunt it, some people can consider it unprofessional and ghetto.

Your hairstyle should be chosen based upon your target audience. Be mindful of what kind of attention you want to attract from your audience. There is nothing wrong with being expressive with your hairstyles unless it takes the focus away from your business. Not all attention is good attention, and sometimes regardless of what type of attention you receive, it can work out for your good. Improving your hair care can also consist of managing fly aways and monitoring unwanted hair. Experiment, get feedback from people that you trust, and don't forget to be yourself when it comes to your hair. Most of all, stay innovative, try new things, and transform your look as your brand transforms.

Be YOU, everyone else is taken.

@iamtaylorsimon #Captivate

A Flawless Face

When we go through our daily routine, one of our goals is to improve our appearance. For most women, cosmetics are essential to enhancing and embellishing features. Relating to your brand, makeup has the potential to add a polished touch to your entire wardrobe. Sticking with neutral tones and hues that compliment your skin is essential to finalizing your look. The audience that you want to attract can define the makeup that you wear. For instance, if you are targeting a more minimalistic audience, applying the simplest makeup look can suffice. On the other hand, if you are trying to find a centric audience, a glam look would be appropriate. Ultimately, how you dress your face can appeal to audience you are trying to attract.

Posture and Personal Branding

People judge within the first 6 seconds of meeting you. How you approach a potential client determines how quickly you can attract finances, opportunities, and divine connections. When it comes to your personal branding, your posture matters. Posture is power and serves as a strong form of communication. Have you ever been captivated by someone with extreme confidence in their posture? From the way they walk, to the way they stand speaks the language of success. They are the kind of people that don't have to fish for attention, because the attention is attracted to them. They don't have to nail their pitch, because their posture and body language speaks for itself.

There is power in your presence and improving your posture amplifies that power. Posture is connected to how you carry yourself. Some people slouch with hunched over shrugged shoulders with their face pointing towards the ground. This frame reveals low self-esteem, lack of ambition, instability, timidity, fear, and absent-mindedness. When you are looking at the ground, instead of looking in the direction you are going, there is a possibility that you could run into a wall. We don't want that! Face your fears head on and walk with focus by lifting your head and shoulders so that you can look like a person who knows where they are going in life.

No matter what comes your way, face your future with fierceness. Doing this conveys self-assurance and embodies a person with strength and sophistication. Even if you have no clue of where you are headed, at least you've postured yourself to evolve in the process of achieving your goals and dreams in life.

Don't let anyone intimidate you into shrinking back into yourself because you are exquisite and extraordinary.

@iamtaylorsimon #Captivate

Mastering your posture involves special attention to the way that you walk across the room. It doesn't matter if you have $10 in your bank account. If you are determined enough, you will walk into a crowd with such confidence and leave with $10,000. Yes my friend, this can happen, but you must be willing to walk it out fearlessly.

To develop a powerful posture, start with the way you enter a room and what you want it to say about you. This will take some time preparing and practicing to convey consistency in your personal brand. Walking gracefully with poise and confidence increases your likeability and approachability. It has also been said that walking properly is good for your health and boosts your self-esteem and confidence. There are plenty of ways that you can appeal your dream clients in your posture.

Here are 10 tips to practice when wanting to improve your posture and presentation of your personal brand:

1. Elongate your body, stand tall and align your head with your spine
2. Chin up and Chest out
3. Shoulders slightly pulled back
4. Tuck your tummy
5. Walk with one foot in front of the other
6. Project your voice and introduce yourself with confidence

7. Keep your eyes looking forward
8. Relax, look natural, and most of all, breath!
9. Take your time, walk with attentiveness, while making yourself available for being approached
10. A smile will go a long way. It says that you are confident, self-assured, and friendly.

Applying these simple tips in your posture will scream confidence. Look at yourself in the mirror and watch your movements. Observe how you stand and pay much attention to the placement of your hands. Keep your eyes on the prize and focus on where you want to go.

Practicing a powerful stance in the presence of others will exude supreme confidence and influence your ability to establish meaningful connections.

Taylor Made Success Tips

• Avoid chipped nail polish or crusted cuticles. Make an extra effort to get manicured or neatly trimmed nails.

• Always carry a pack of mints to keep your mouth fresh when communicating with other people.

• Eliminate unpleasant odors by wearing deodorant and sparse perfume or cologne. Don't overwhelm people with loud scents.

Use Your **BIG** Platform
to Ressurect
BIG Dreams

yes!

You Were Born to Be A
Superhero
for everyone else...

SECRET
Strategy
#7

#7

Master Your Message

Your brand needs a voice. Your voice needs to be heard. You have a message. You have a story to tell. And guess what? No one else can tell it better than you can. No one can relive the uncomfortable and most unbearable moments like you can. No one can see what you have seen unless you are willing to share every aching scene. No one can feel what you feel unless you are willing to express it despite how you feel. When you become brave enough to unwrap the most avoided things, you will escape the grasp of fear that has been trying to keep you from the greater things that life has to offer you.

The fuel that keeps the vision of your brand going depends on the depths of the message that you choose to share with the masses. Your message plays an important role in the marketplace. The marketplace is not just a place where people shop; it is an environment where services are exchanged. The marketplace is where people seek safety, solutions, and systems. The marketplace is where people find community. A community where they can find like-minded individuals that can relate to their humanity.

Your audience is waiting to share their triumphs and communicate their sufferings. They are waiting for the opportunity to launch their dreams. But they need a voice. Your tribe needs a voice that will guide them towards achieving victories unimaginable. They need you to serve them towards a lifestyle that they've never seen before. The challenge is not selling your product; the challenge is in connecting and convicting your audience in a strategic way that will keep them coming back for more.

Yes, the secret to success in business is not just about the art of checks and balances, it is about servicing the people and creating a community. It is your responsibility to create a climate of likeness that makes others, who may not know you, welcome to join you on the journey towards ultimate freedom in life and in business.

Effective branding in business is driven by strong communities that are constantly fed with solutions that will leave a legacy not just for your family but also for their own. If you didn't know, your brand cannot survive on door-to-door marketing. Over time, innovation has called for a deeper level of connectivity with our dream clients. To keep the people's attention you have to speak about what matters most. Your message is what makes your brand matter the most. It is what will impact and inspire your audience outside of the salesy talk. Your story isn't meant to be sold, it's meant to be given freely as a gift. Depending on how deep you are willing to go will determine the believability and genuineness of that gift. Ultimately, your story doesn't belong to you. That's why it's a gift. Regardless of the dirty, filthy, baggage that wraps your story, your story is what your tribe will find hope and healing in. Your message belongs to the world and the world needs to hear it.

Right now, as you are reading this, I want you to take a deep breath and prepare your heart to relinquish the fortress. Your story is your fuel, not your fortress. It is time to relinquish the comfortable safety net that has been holding your dreams hostage. To go higher, you must go deeper. Don't get me wrong, sharing your truth is going to cost you something. Moving from mediocrity to greatness requires sacrifice. Are you up for the challenge? This secret is about telling an unforgettable story that will expand your influence, elevate your outcome, and maximize your ability to captivate the masses.

You hold the recipe of prosperity and freedom in the story that you choose to share.

@iamtaylorsimon #Captivate

THE FORMULA

Often time, people decide with their emotions then justify their decision with their logic. The formula to mastering your message is triggering those emotions and challenging them to take action that they cannot resist. The best way to get people to open up to you is to open up to them. People like to hear from people that are just like them. People don't care about how much you know until they know how much you care. And most of all, they want to hear from people they can trust. They don't want to know what you do more than why you do it. Without your why, your what plummets. And if your why does not connect with their soul, your message loses its power. As small business owners, public speakers, authors, entrepreneurs, creatives, and global leaders, your story must stick. No matter what industry you are in, your message will allow you to reach a demographic of individuals that you would have never imagined were waiting for you. Mastering your message is meant to be challenging, because if it doesn't challenge you it doesn't grow you.

To activate this growth, I have created a signature story telling and message mastery system called **The Soar System**™ that will take you to new heights in your messaging and help you to land with ease. So many of us settle for the pitch, but the pitch won't stick unless it is stitched to their hearts.

In this system, you must be willing to use the thing that attempted to make you sink in disappointment, shame, or failure and craft a story that will prepare you to soar into a lifetime of limitless opportunities. This signature system will challenge you to talk about who you are now, who you were then, and why anyone should care. In the end, you will give them an opportunity to create a pivotal life-altering decision to take action towards their future. If you land effectively, your audience will feel an unbreakable urgency to convert into a loyal paying customer.

I have learned that major media platforms usually stay on the phone with you no more than 12 minutes. They won't listen unless you become vulnerable. The key is to earn more time past the time that was given to you. Ultimately, it's about taking advantage of one opportunity and getting an invitation back. The secret to earning more time with your audience is by giving the people more of you. Believe me, your story will open doors to the degree in which you unpack it.

Are you ready to unpack the unspoken? To soar in your messaging, you must be willing to dig through the messy things in order to unlock the miraculous. If you allow yourself to evolve through this entire storytelling strategy, you will witness immediate improvement and transformation in your speaking, your business, and in yourself. Get ready to soar!

The Signature Storytelling + Message Mastery System: The Soar System™

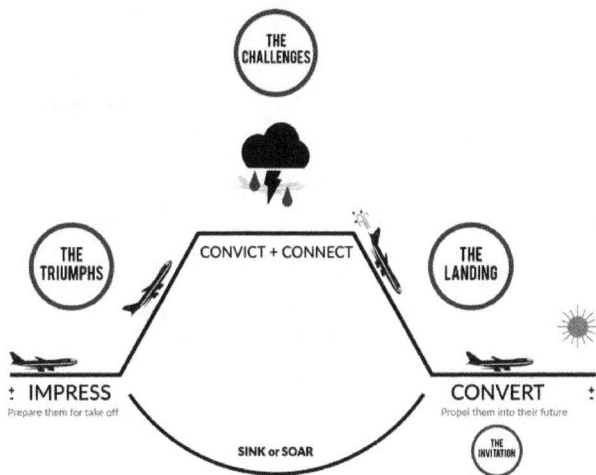

Phase 1: Impress with your Triumphs

In the first phase of **The Soar System**™, your mission is to prepare your audience for take off. The way you begin will determine the return you will receive in the end. This is your spotlight moment to take center stage and WOW your audience with your impressive triumphs. This is your chance to be the superhero. If you didn't know already, you were born to be a superhero for everyone else. You were born with abilities that have and will continue to bring you great success. But what is success when you cannot share it with others?

This phase is where you explain who you are now. The mighty you. The heavily sought after expert, master, coach, teacher, influencer, strategist, or speaker. The one that is in high-demand. The person that everyone loves. I call this The Mega You. Building momentum and motivation with The Mega You proves that you are credible and trustworthy. Your audience needs to be convinced that you are qualified to share insight and information with them. If no one has said your bio prior to you getting on stage, take advantage of this moment to emphasize your impressive accomplishments and achievements.

I know that some of you may be thinking, "I don't have any super impressive achievements or prestigious awards." Before you go any further with that thought, I want you to think about the mini wins that led you to any big wins that you have achieved in life. Depending on what is most relevant to your audience, you can share full ride scholarships to college, celebrate that you are "building a multi-million dollar company" (you may not be the "billionaire" yet, but you are well on your way, so this is definitely something to celebrate), became a parent, or share the joys of the time you won a juggling contest. Any wins that you can think about, I want you to write them down and celebrate them. There are so many things to celebrate; it is up to you to see them as such.

When you celebrate you, others will too.

@iamtaylorsimon #Captivate

Write down 5 Personal and Professional Wins to Celebrate

Personal Wins

1._____

_____

2._____

_____

3._____

_____

4._____

_____

5._____

_____

Professional Wins

1._____

_____

2._____

_____

3._____

_____

4._____

_____

5._____

_____

Of course, no one wants to listen to an obnoxious bragger that talks about themself all day. The key to mastering this phase is to practice talking comfortably about your wins from a place of service rather than a place of self-centeredness. As I've stated before, you are the hero. Superheroes never forget that it is about serving the people even while being in a place of mega-influence.

You are the voice to let them know that nothing is impossible. This is your chance to let them know, as one of my mentors, Jonathan Sprinkles says, *IT CAN BE DONE*. Most importantly, you must be available to tell them how. As you take the stage, you are the dream restorer, the hope giver, and the passion liberator. You are the victor on a mission to bring healing to the victims. Who you are now, is who they aspire to be.

Use your big platform to resurrect big dreams.

@iamtaylorsimon #Captivate

Your Motivation Activator

Make this moment an occasion filled with high energy and excitement. Get creative and come up with your own signature motivation activators. Your *Motivation Activator* can be a joyous chant or cheer that stimulates movement in your audience. Design the experience by entering the room to your favorite song and encourage your audience to join in on the excitement. This strategy can give your moment a unique personality. Your options to captivating creativity are endless. Start thinking about some unique ways to get your audience moved, motivated, and making some noise! A highly motivated entrance activates high conversions.

You were born to be a superhero for everyone else.

@iamtaylorsimon #Captivate

Phase 2: Convict + Connect with your Challenges

This is your changing moment. It's time to speak from the heart. Phase 2 is your opportunity to speak from your convictions and connect with your challenges. This moment is where you share your fears, failures, and pitfalls. This moment is where you explain how you got from here to there. This moment is where you give yourself permission to speak the unspoken and write the unwritten. What you have had to face in life is rare. You have not always been the champion, because before you were the victor, you were the victim to somebody or something.

Not many people have an opportunity to share their message until it's too late. But if you do it right, you will be able to soar across cultural boundaries, political boundaries, and even religious boundaries. As you transition from celebrating *The Mega You*, you will now flow into sharing *The Mini You*. *The Mini You* is who I'd like to call the antagonist, victim, or "wanna be" before the "somebody".

Flowing into this human side of you can begin with the phrase, "It wasn't always this way.."

Now it doesn't always need to be this phrase, but this is just a start to get you going. Yes, you have not always been the CEO of a multi-million dollar corporation. You have not always been a best selling author. And you have not always had successful relationships. Catch my drift? Everyone wants to be the hero, but no one wants to unmask the one with a little start and a big heart. Unless you were born into a well-off family, you have experienced some turbulence in life. Even so, you may have had all the success in the world, but was still taxed with difficult moments. In today's world, transparency inspires. Whether you know it or not, your transparency will reward you beyond what you can comprehend. Vulnerability builds credibility. People thrive off of your blood, sweat, and tears. Why? Because they are always searching for connection. With this connection, they will feel convicted to overcome. Your connection through your challenges creates community. This is very important.

If you are talking about finances, talk about that, if you are talking about relationships, talk about it. If you are talking about confidence, give it all you've got. This system gives you the relationship with your audience. They need to see themselves through your shoes. They need somewhere to belong. They need to know that they are not alone and that it took one person (you), to be brave enough to speak the unspoken.

In this moment, do whatever you need to do to paint the picture, paint the pain, and unpackage your problems. Don't demystify the problems you have faced. Every season and every second of your life is valuable down to the very last detail. Always be clear and unapologetic. Take them into the room, down the hall, and through the conversation. Paint the moment so vividly as if they were there. Invite them into your childhood, take them around your neighborhood block, and drive them back home.

Successful stories expose the highlight reels. When you are talking with your audience, give them an experience that will take their breath away. Take them through the highs and the lows, the yeses and the nos. Welcome them into the all time lows of your journey towards prosperity. Of course, share what you are most comfortable with. But avoid taking up real estate in your comfort zone. Setting up camp in your comfort zone is the recipe for delay. Without the challenges in your life, you wouldn't be the champion that you are today. It was through those turbulences that you have found the greatest life lessons. Because of the mistakes and mishaps, you are now fully equipped to be the coach, the teacher, or the leader you've always dreamed of becoming. You may not have had many struggles or challenges. You may be somewhere in the middle or beyond. But there is always a way to find common ground with your audience and it takes much courage to take it there.

Your turbulence becomes a turbo-boost for someone else's victory.

@iamtaylorsimon #Captivate

Your challenges have the innate ability to captivate the hearts and minds of your audience. Once you have given them more of you, they will respond with "they get me". Dig deep and be authentic in your approach to share a story that not only reveals the best parts of you, but the unusual parts of you.

The best speakers are the best storytellers. So do your research, find the pain in the lives of your audience and connect a story that relates to that same pain.

Relive the pain, relieve the pain, and reap richly off of the pain. When you relive the moment, you will relieve them of unnecessary pain and in return, you will reap greatly off of it. Study your story and find new ways to deliver it. Connect with the people and they will deliver the cash that will help you make a greater impact. Show them how you came from incapable to unstoppable. Teach them how to no longer be the victim of their circumstances in order to become the victor. Convict them to make some changes and provide solutions to initiate that change.

Your message is uncommon, unmatched, and unduplicated. Your story is your super power. Your truth is one of the greatest gifts that you've got. Don't get rid of the "wanna be" now that you've become a "somebody". If it wasn't for the old you, the new you wouldn't have a story to tell. Don't be afraid to tell it. When you master your challenges, you will have nothing to hide, nothing to protect, and nothing to defend. During this process, you must be willing to unhook yourself from anyone or anything that would prevent you from being you.

In this defining moment, don't let your challenges be your crutch, let it be your crown that symbolizes strength, endurance, and determination. Let it be known that in order to live the dream, you have to be inconvenienced. You can't get the dream staying on the inside of your problems. You have to get out and go through in order to get to the other side of your problems. There is so much power in that. Share your story while you're still around to tell it. Your message is important to the lively hood of other people. Allow yourself to be, build relationship with your audience, and create a moment that no one will ever forget.

You must be willing to go places that others wouldn't go, say things that others won't say, and do things that others wouldn't do in order to become the man or woman you have always wanted to be. – Lisa Nichols

Convert them with your Landing

Now that you've made it through the storm, it's time to drive them with your why and empower them with your how. Your why is what gives your story purpose and meaning. Applying your how is what gives your message value and vision. Think about why you do what you do, especially after all of the challenges that you've gone through. Consider why you believe that you are called to serve. Share what inspires you to do what you do.

This phase of the system gives you the opportunity to unpackage the story and shine the light on the hidden insight. Provide them with your "undiscovered revelation". Make it easy to comprehend; yet powerful enough to impact. Let your audience know that you made it through the storm and this is how. Give them your "secret sauce" and "never-seen-before" strategies and lessons. Your best strategies, tips, lessons, and how-tos is what they want to hear and ultimately what got them in their seats. I like to call these signature solutions.

This is what gives The Mega You, credit, credibility and support. Think about it. It's great hearing about The Mega You, but people want to know HOW YOU DID IT. How you overcame fear and doubt, how you were able to have 2 best selling books, how you were able to earn $100,000 in 10 days, how you got your first million in your first year of launching your business, how you became debt free in 2 years, or how you lost over 100 pounds in 90 days. Whatever your how is, this is where you land it. Your audience came with a problem, and your job is to seal the deal with an unexpected solution.

Here are some questions to think about when landing:

- Why should they care about your story?
- Why does it matter to them anyway?
- What can they apply to their life that will change them for the rest of their lives?
- What does your audience need?
- What will be the most valuable content that they will benefit from the most?

Invite them to Take Undeniable Action

Here is where you test their captivation level. If you captivated them well with your message, they will feel compelled to do what you want them to do and go where you need them to go. Once you've landed them with your signature solutions, now its time to propel them into taking action. This phase is where you invite them to take a personal and profitable CTA or call-to-action. The personal CTA are action steps that will bring your audience personal benefits. This can be things that they can apply with accountability and assurance. The profitable CTA is what gets them to convert. Essentially, it is what gets them into your email list, next class, or purchasing your book. Consider using an "Impossible to Resist" Freebie to make the invitation more inviting. This is what converts them to producing profitability in your business.

I believe that each of these are important because it provides them accountability and earns you potential clients. The ultimate goal is to inspire them to take action. A loving invitation to take action that makes them feel inspired to choose and not feel like "if I don't do it I'm wrong". Make this invitation exclusive and undeniable. Give them the option and not the demand. Don't force their hand, hold their hand to an invitation that they can't deny.

Your income determines your outcome. What you put into it will determine what you will get out of it.

@iamtaylorsimon #Captivate

Captivate

to make a

Difference

& NOT JUST TO

Make a Profit

CAPTIVATE
Millions

CAPTIVATE
Millions

*Captivate to make a difference,
and not just to make a profit.*

In this book, you are allowed to say no, you are allowed to let go, and you are allowed to try new things. Do what works for you, test it, and apply it. The truth to these secrets is that not all of them may work for you. But the most fulfilling "risk" is taking a chance to do something that you've never done before in order to achieve a different outcome in your business and lifestyle.

I challenge you to captivate millions.

I challenge you to go beyond what's been comfortable to you.

From the moment you press play on Facebook live to walking into a networking event.

People are waiting to greet you.
People are waiting to see you.
People are waiting to know you.

From the moment you open your mouth, you will captivate people. This book was meant to teach you how to build a captivating brand that will draw millions beyond the dream clients. It was meant to help you attract infinite resources, divine connections, and cash to fund your passions. It was meant to give you hope, courage, confidence and belief that will open doors no one can close.

The key is to captivate to make a difference, and not just to make a profit.

Don't just tell them who you are, show them who you are.

As an entrepreneur, business owner, speaker, author, leader, or creative, now is the time unfold your captivating capabilities to attract your dream clients and move your business, career, and lifestyle in a positive and profitable direction!

Use these tools right where you are to stand out, build brand awareness, position yourself as an expert in your industry, earn more respect, gain exposure, and dominate your industry.

So many brands are competing for attention, but yours will have the main spot. As you grow your business beyond where you are, marketing your brand in a captivating way can open doors to global influence. *Start today by showing up, dressing the part, being the part, delivering consistently, serving confidently, and engaging with excitement!*

Notes

https://ryanbattles.com/post/defining-customer-avatars

http://www.referralcandy.com/blog/customer-seduction-make-customers-love-brand-infographic/

http://www.lifehack.org/articles/communication/17-tips-help-you-expand-your-influence.html

https://eventup.com/blog/2016/12/21/how-to-be-the-most-interesting-person-at-a-networking-event/

http://rich-page.com/website-optimization/how-to-better-captivate-and-engage-your-homepage-visitors-in-less-than-5-seconds/

http://www.inboundmarketingagents.com/inbound-marketing-agents-blog/bid/345449/6-elements-of-outstanding-homepage-design

https://www.inc.com/wanda-thibodeaux/being-successful-could-come-down-to-changing-up-your-hair-according-to-science.html

https://blog.hubspot.com/marketing/visual-con-
tent-marketing-infographic#sm.0001yh7eug8wwepbz-
5412rgsuaiwp

A dynamic celebrity brand designer, the World's #1 Captivate Coach, vision architect, author, transformational speaker, and spiritual leader, Taylor Simon is committed to helping dreamers, leaders, and entrepreneurs unlock their infinite potential, conquer their fears, and stand in their greatness. She teaches people looking to design and launch a Taylor Made Lifestyle while elevating their influence, income, and inner beliefs for personal and professional prosperity. From a lemonade stand to becoming the CEO and Founder of a branding and marketing agency called Divine Desires and Taylor Made Lifestyle & Design, Taylor specializes in developing the entrepreneurial spirit in every big dreamer that aspires to achieve their divine desires. Her passion is to motivate, equip, and transform individuals to think BIG and dream BIGGER to build a life long legacy for generations to come.

She has a distinguished ability to take anyone from undiscovered to unforgettable with her out of the box strategy and uncommon approach to helping people leverage the ordinary and transform it into something extraordinary. Through the many hats that she wears, Taylor is devoted to challenging others to fearlessly, authentically, confidently, and strategically stand out and deliver their message and brand to the world.

Taylor has hosted many sold out events, frequently empower hundreds of people in seminars, conferences, and events, and have had multiple television and radio appearances around the nation. Currently residing in Fort Worth, Texas, Taylor is a devoted wife to Alford Simon, the founder of a women and young girl's nonprofit organization, loves to sing, cook exotic dishes and is passionate about health and fitness.

Learn More About Taylor Simon at
www.iamtaylorsimon.com

Connect with Taylor

@iamtaylorsimon
Taylor Simon

Book Taylor

info@iamtaylorsimon.com
www.iamtaylorsimon.com

DIVINE
DESIRES
BRANDING & MARKETING AGENCY

ELEVATE YOUR BRAND &
Deliver in Excellence

WHO WE ARE

We are a full-service creative agency committed to using innovative marketing strategies, dynamic creative communication and premium branding to generate increased brand awareness, engage and convert new consumers, and promote ongoing social traffic.

WHY CHOOSE US

Choosing us is choosing greatness. We know what it's like to want more in life. More visibility, increased engagement, extra clients, greater wealth, expanded reach, and an upgraded look. Does any of this sounds familiar to you? Our Divine Desire is to help you look better, dream bigger, and achieve greater. We guarantee that your dream and vision is destined to thrive with us.

OUR SERVICES

BRAND DEVELOPMENT   GRAPHIC + PRINT DESIGN
MARKETING   BOOK PUBLISHING
SOCIAL MEDIA + PR
WEB DESIGN + DEVELOPMENT
COACHING + CONSULTING
PHOTOGRAPHY

CONTACT US

P. 888-371-9990 | INFO@DIVINEDESIRES.ORG
WWW.DIVINEDESIRES.ORG | @DIVINE_DESIRES